WISDOM *from the* WOODS

NAVIGATING LIFE'S UNEXPECTED CHALLENGES

Virginia Gilmore
Duane Trammell

TRAMMELL MCGEE-COOPER AND ASSOCIATES, INC.
Dal'

D1114461

For more information please contact:
Sophia Transformative Leadership Partners
office@sophiapartners.org
Trammell McGee-Cooper and Associates, Inc.
duane@amca.com

Cover and Text Design by Suzanne Pustejovsky Design, Austin, Texas
Composition by Timm Chamberlain, Dallas, Texas
Editing by Deborah Costenbader, Austin, Texas

Library of Congress Control Number 2020908777
ISBN 978-1-7350647-0-3

*I, **Virginia Gilmore**, dedicate this book to
my beloved husband, Jim Gilmore,
whose love and partnership, including all of his support
with this book, bless my life every day
in too many ways to measure . . .
and to my children, Rob and Ginger, and my grandchildren,
Max, Will, Wes, and Ruby Virginia, whom I love with all my heart.
It is my hope and intention for this book to be a helpful resource
for them in meaningful ways through the
unexpected challenges in their own lives.*

*I, **Duane Trammell**, dedicate my part in this book to
my husband, Steven Pace.
Through thirty-three years of relationship, we have experienced
many transitions. Coming out to family, job losses,
loss of many of our friends through AIDS,
illnesses of our aging parents, the loss of one of our brothers,
deaths of our parents, and the heartbreaking
loss of our friend and business partner, Ann McGee-Cooper.
Through all of these transitions, Steven has stood beside me,
supporting me, holding my heart, and helping me to weather
the changes and see the hope on the other side.*

CONTENTS

AUTHORS

Virginia Gilmore, L.H.D

Ginny's experience with her father and two brothers in the fourth-generation family manufacturing business, Kaytee Products Incorporated, served as the foundation for her continued calling of servant leadership. Focusing on the importance of leadership as relationship, she continued to learn through forming teaching and learning communities for research and service. In 2002, she founded Sophia Foundation, with the vision of creating caring community through its mission of supporting the spirit, dignity, and potential of every person through unique leadership programs and collaborative partnerships. In 2009, Marian University recognized her with a Doctor of Humane Letters in honor of her work in servant leadership in the community and the world. Ginny is a facilitator for the Virtual Servant Leadership Learning Community® program which she co-founded with Ann McGee-Cooper and Deborah Welch in 2009. She focuses on learning, writing, facilitating, and mentoring others who are navigating change in their work and their lives. Ginny especially treasures spending time with her husband, Jim Gilmore, and her family, including her four grandchildren Max, Will, Wes, and Ruby Virginia.

Duane Trammell, M.Ed.

Duane Trammell is President and Founding Partner of Trammell McGee-Cooper and Associates, Inc. He has been a writer, presenter, and thought-leader in the field of servant leadership since 1982. Duane enjoyed a thirty-five-year partnership with Dr. Ann McGee-Cooper, until her passing in 2016, and participated in her early research on genius/giftedness, combining it with Robert Greenleaf's concepts on servant leadership. As a business educator and leadership development specialist, Duane's forte is designing and delivering participant-based learning. Duane enjoys writing, researching, and developing materials in servant leadership. He has co-authored *Time Management for Unmanageable People, You Don't Have to Go Home from Work Exhausted!; Being the Change: Profiles from Our Servant Leadership Learning Community; Awakening Your Sleeping Genius:*

A Journaling Approach to Servant Leadership; and *The Art of Coaching for Servant Leadership,* co-authored with Deborah Welch and Ann McGee-Cooper. Duane holds a M.Ed. in Gifted Education and Supervision as well as post Master's studies with international thought-leaders. Educational awards include "Dallas Teacher of the Year," "The Ross Perot Award for Teaching Excellence," and "Outstanding Teachers in Texas." He also received the CoreNet's 2016 Industry Excellence Award—Leadership Development for the project team who built the New Parkland Hospital, a 1.3 billion-dollar project in Dallas, Texas. Duane enjoys living in downtown Dallas with his husband of thirty-three years, Steven Pace.

Virginia Gilmore   Duane Trammell

MEET THE AUTHORS, WATCH VIDEOS AND MORE AT
WisdomfromtheWoodsBook.com

FOREWORD

by GARY J. BOELHOWER

I've had the honor of being a learning partner with Ginny Gilmore through many adventures and transitions. To walk beside Ginny and deeply witness her life of service has been a profound gift that has brought me joy, inspiration, and hope.

My connection with Duane Trammell has been in the context of gatherings focused on servant leadership. I deeply appreciate his skills and the heart he brings to his work. Although there are many rich dimensions to the stories Ginny and Duane tell, I want to focus on what I see as the most important — the call to silence.

WE LIVE IN AN AGE OF UNPRECEDENTED SPEED AND ACCESS to information. We are inundated with stimuli constantly — tweets, texts, emails, phone calls, news feeds, data and analysis, videos, podcasts, etc. As these rushing streams of information wash over us, we are asked to work faster and faster; to somehow digest it all instantaneously, and come up with the next best process or product or personal decision. In this context, the call to silence is countercultural, challenging, and absolutely critical.

If we do not enter the silence, we cannot access the most fundamental source of our inner wisdom — our heart or soul or true self. Parker Palmer in *Let Your Life Speak* says, "The soul speaks its truth only under quiet, inviting and trustworthy conditions." He compares the soul or true self to a wild animal that simply won't reveal itself if you "go crashing through the woods, shouting for the creature to come out."[1] To listen to our inner self, we need silence. To create time and space for that silence is a courageous act, even if it is a minute before a feedback session with a valued employee, or an hour as we discern the direction forward, or a day as we take stock of our lives.

It is often easier to rely on external sources of information and wisdom than to take the journey inward, easier to interrogate another expert, set up another taskforce, read another book, or go for another run with my earbuds in so I can listen to a recent podcast that is sure to make everything clear. Of course, external wisdom and expertise are very important. However, that cannot substitute for the wisdom that comes from the heart and soul of my true self. To access this wisdom of the soul, this center of my unique person, requires silence and patience.

*If we do not consult our own soul,
we never know what we believe,*

what is of central importance to us, or who we really want to become. Without connecting to our inner wisdom, we follow the crowd or listen to the loudest voice or shape our lives to someone else's expectation. When we do not take the time to listen to the inner teacher, we end up living a life that is not really our own. To live an inauthentic life takes a great toll on our body and spirit, and on others around us, because we are more apt to show up in our relationships with insecurity and anger, frustration, and a lack of compassion.

The courage to create time and space for silence is fundamental to being true to ourselves, to living with a sense of authenticity, and to being a good leader at home, in our communities, and at work. I hope Ginny's and Duane's stories will encourage you to claim the silence, to carve out time in your hectic lives for deep listening to your own true self. I invite you to take at least a little bit of time each day to slip into the silence. Perhaps you can get up 15 minutes before the rest of the household and sit with a cup of coffee on the deck or stay up 30 minutes after everyone has gone to bed and light a candle in your living room or take 10 minutes after your lunch break for a brief walk with no earbuds.

You might imagine lowering your body into the lake of silence; it will accept you with its total embrace. It will not ask for a password. It won't even care about mistakes you have made. You cannot keep any secrets from the silence; you will be simply all you are, whole and entire. You cannot know the future and you cannot change the past, but in the moment of silence you can be fully present right here and right now. The silence won't ask you to prove anything; it will simply take you in. Use the rhythm of the stars and the stories of the constellations to know your way forward. Listen to your wilderness, to the calling of your soul. In this kind heartbeat is all the life you need. This breath, this step forward toward the feast.

It may take some practice to quiet all the other voices that are constantly running around in our heads. Don't try to push anything away or reach for anything that isn't there. Simply embrace what the silence brings. Notice what comes up in your mind, your body, your spirit. Simply listen deeply for the voice of your inner teacher. Sometimes it helps to journal or focus on your breathing or sound a gong to call your attention. For some, sitting with their back straight and their feet on the ground creates the energy to pay close attention. Sometimes lying on the ground with your body connected to the earth is helpful. For others, the rhythm of walking, the swing of arms and legs in their sockets, connects them to a deeper rhythm in their lives. Experiment and find what works for you.

You may whisper your name in the silence and listen for others saying their names as well. You might hear each of our small swirl of hopes and prayers spiraling out like Sufi robes in the common dance. You might hear hands rise up in the world's song, all of us dancing together on this tiny rock with fire in its soul, spinning through the grand galaxies with mercy and wonder.

Let the silence enter and do its work.
Listen to the heart
of your deepest longing.

PREFACE

DUANE TRAMMELL

We have all had those moments in life when our worlds are turned upside down. Our job is eliminated and we find ourselves frantic about the mortgage; a long-term loving relationship breaks apart; or we get the news—"it's cancer." Events happen that cause our legs to buckle, our stomachs to turn queasy, and our heads to spin. Tsunami change can do that to us. We feel so grounded one moment, and in the next, it feels like the earth is swallowing us.

Any life transition serious enough to shake us at our core requires not only small adjustments in our mental, emotional, and spiritual lives, but an all-out strategic focus of both the mind and the heart. Though I have experienced many changes in my life, I wasn't prepared for what happened in 2015.

Flashback to 1977

In 1977, when Jimmy Carter was president, the first Star Wars was creating lines at movie theaters, and disco balls were whirling to the sounds of the Bee Gees, I graduated from college with a shiny new teaching degree. With a cardboard box of bulletin board supplies in hand, I started my teaching career in a low-income neighborhood in the Dallas Independent School District. It was difficult. I replaced a teacher who had been fired for incompetence, and the class was unruly. I was an inexperienced twenty-one-year-old white boy in a black neighborhood and had much to learn, not only about teaching, but cultural differences as well. The first year of teaching was disappointing to me, and I wanted to give up and look for other work. As the school year closed, I noticed an ad for teachers interested in a new talented and gifted program. I applied for a position and was accepted.

During the summer months I attended special training classes, and the program administrators assigned me to a school in another low-income area. But I felt energized and more prepared this time. As a part of this program we received ongoing training and development, and I met Dr. Ann McGee-Cooper. She was a creative spirit with a shopping bag of materials, and she captured my heart. I used her suggested teaching techniques with great success which led to three teaching awards—"Dallas Teacher of the Year," "The Ross Perot Award for Excellence in Teaching," and "One of the Three Best Teachers in Texas." After five years of teaching, Ann invited me to leave the school district and join her in creating a consulting company. We worked first with teachers and school districts, but realized if significant change was to happen in education, we would need to gain the attention of business. Corporate people were on school boards, funded initiatives, and influenced education. We created a program for talented and gifted business people.

For the next thirty-five years, Ann and I worked together traveling the world with our leadership development programs. We were a perfect partnership, balancing each other's thinking and strengths. We had fun working together and writing five books. Our plan was to continue until we retired or couldn't work any longer. But something happened to spoil that plan. Despite an exceedingly healthy lifestyle, Ann was diagnosed with breast cancer that quickly morphed into stage 4 cancer. We made her cancer a part of our business routine. I went to her doctors' appointments and sat with her in the chemo transfusion room, planning our next business program. This worked for four years. But something was worrying me in the summer of 2015. I sensed troubling times were ahead. I put in place the business processes we needed for a transition, yet I didn't feel emotionally or spiritually prepared. I was already grieving the loss of Ann from our business and as my best friend, and I knew that I needed to work on myself at a much deeper level. I didn't know where to start and needed a process or a plan to guide me.

The Heart Connection

I met Ginny Gilmore around 2001 at the Robert K. Greenleaf Annual Conference for Servant Leadership. Through the years we shared an occasional conference dinner but had minimal contact. In 2009, we co-created the Virtual Servant Leadership Learning Community® (VSLLC®) with the Sophia Foundation and Ginny co-facilitated sessions with Deborah Welch and Ann McGee-Cooper. I joined that program as a co-facilitator for a special group targeted to business participants, but Ginny's group and mine were separate. We were acquaintances with a mutual respect for each other's roles. All of that dramatically changed in July 2015.

I believe that a divine intervention occurred that July. I was in a place of need and so was Ginny Gilmore. In a casual email exchange with her, something happened. We both know the exact day that a deep friendship was born. It was August 2, 2015, through brief words of condolence surrounding the heartbreaking death of Ginny's neighbor. A few weeks passed and then on September 3rd, our friendship was birthed through an exchange of the heart. We stepped through the veil of polite distance and crossed into sharing honest and intense feelings that the death of a friend brought up for each of us. Both of us risked sharing from the depth of our souls about the fears, uncertainty, and transitions happening in our own lives. For the next few weeks, we emailed several times a week . . . helping each other make sense of transitions we found ourselves navigating.

I remember being afraid, confused, unsure of myself, yet knowing that I needed to strengthen my resolve about the future. I did what I knew to do from a business perspective, but my heart and spirit were troubled. Ann and I were still doing a few programs together, but my intuition told me something was looming, and I needed to get on with the transition of our company. As Ginny and I talked about this, she remarked that she had written a piece that might help me. She explained that this wasn't her first major transition. Twenty years earlier, Ginny's life was turned upside down with a series of events, and her future was even more unclear at that time. She offered to mail me a copy of "The Healing Journey" (HJ).

One October evening it arrived, and I immediately started reading. I could not put the story down and finished it in one sitting. It was exactly the help I needed to begin my own journey. I had been floundering, not quite knowing where to start the inner work that I needed to make this transition. Ginny's story was a complete picture of how to do this; she shared her intuitive process and how she found peace and direction for the future.

I quickly emailed Ginny and expressed how much her story was helping me. For the next ten months we began a deep dialogue centered on various parts of HJ and how we were navigating the major transitions in our lives.

VIRGINIA GILMORE

In that moment, everything shifts. Life can change in a moment!

Nothing is ever the same. Experiences like this have happened to me several times in my life. What I have learned over the years, especially through my experience in 1996, is that there are ways I can support myself through this kind of deep change. I have also grown to know that Mystery is in charge, and anything can happen. What matters is to be attuned to what is unfolding during times like this. Ribbons of experiences unfold and offer guideposts and lamplights to the rest of one's life.

Unexpected Connections Can Forge Change

I was in the second year of a similar transformational transition in July of 2015. I was smack in the middle of a shift that was calling for me to change my life. After founding Sophia Foundation in 2002, it became clear to me that I was being

Ginny and Duane in Door County, Wisconsin – October 2016

called to a different way to live and to serve. I was entrenched in a slow process of releasing my leadership role and connection with the Sophia Foundation. Supported by a spiritual guide, I was making my way forward, trusting that I would be led as I had been other times in my life. I had no idea where I was going as I navigated in my lifeboat each day, trying to find the way. That's when it happened, right in the midst of experiencing the loss of a friend and neighbor in my Door County (Wisconsin) community. Duane Trammell's caring words of friendship watered my cracked-open heart when I returned from the funeral. I wrote back and thanked him. When he received my message, he felt called to continue this connection at a time when his own life was shaken by the cancer diagnosis given to his longtime friend and working partner of thirty-five years. He wrote back. Thus began a friendship in which I have been able to hear my heart and find my way. When I sent Duane a copy of "The Healing Journey" that I had written twenty years ago, I had no idea that, as a result of his reading, it would become a guiding light for both of us.

OUT OF OUR OWN JOURNEYS OF DEEP CHANGE and trans-formation, we offer you this portal into "The Healing Journey," with our hope that it will offer you encouragement and support for your own journeys of change.

Part One

THE HEALING JOURNEY

VIRGINIA GILMORE

Introduction

VIRGINIA GILMORE

May 1995 REPRESENTED A MARKER FOR CHANGE IN MY LIFE. My youngest child, Ginger, graduated from high school. My role as mother changed. I had prepared ahead for that transition for at least a year. Little did I know that this would be the first of many life changes that year.

Approximately one month later, my second husband and I separated, rather abruptly. Although I expected that the marriage might end, I was totally unprepared for it to happen at that time. Within a few weeks, the divorce proceedings were underway.

By December of that same year, the third change process began. After participating in a family business as co-owner and executive for seventeen years, it became apparent that the time had arrived for me to leave my role as vice president

of customer service. I had long awaited the opportunity to have
other choices in my life. In particular, I wanted to focus on my
spirituality and share what I learned with others. Since I had
never completed my undergraduate degree, I had unfinished
business there and an opportunity to move into the career of my
choice. Yearning for this choice, I made the decision to leave the
position that had required a significant amount of my attention for
so many years.

So, there I was—no children at home, no husband, and no job!
Besides that, I was about to celebrate my fiftieth birthday. There
was no model in my family for all of this. Although I knew I was
making a good decision, I was lost and frightened.

After a summer with my children at home and the finalization
of details as a result of leaving my job, I was tired. I longed for rest
and space. I could clearly hear my need for separation from all the
responsibility, except the big one—the responsibility for myself.

A summer weekend trip to Door County, Wisconsin, showed
me the answer. After spending a peaceful weekend there with a
friend, I planned a two-month sabbatical for September and
October in a setting that reminded me of a sacred time from my
childhood. I was ready for a new journey of silence and solitude.
I could no longer find excuses to wait. I had come face to face with
my own heart.

It was time to meet my soul!

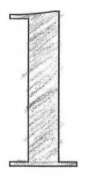

The Call

How might it have been different for you . . .
If someone had been able to see that you were taking
the first tiny baby step toward feeling your own feelings,
of knowing that you saw life differently from those around you.
If you had been helped to experience your own uniqueness,
to feel the excitement of sensing, for the very first time,
your own awareness of life. What if someone had helped you
to own all of this . . . to own your own life?

How might it be different for you?

It is often, finally, a woman's own pain and sadness
that make her change her life. Finally it is impossible
to deny her feelings any longer.

—Judith Duerk
Circles of Stones[2]

5

Nature was beckoning to us!

It was mid-June in 1996 when my friend Loretta and I stood looking at beautiful Lake Michigan in Newport State Park, just north of Sister Bay, Wisconsin. Loretta and I had planned this weekend retreat for a couple of months. She needed some quiet relief from the overruling stress of corporate life, and I needed to take a break from the continuum of change that had found its way into my life. Besides that, my retirement lunch was coming up the following week—a lunch recognizing my departure from my family company where I had worked for the last seventeen years. Yes, we had enough justification between the two of us to support this weekend away, pulled by the call of the Northland in Wisconsin's beautiful Door County (referred to as "Door" from hence forward). We were both anxious to experience the water, the woods, and the crisp, clear air, and we welcomed the chance to reconnect with the freedom of nature.

"Go to Newport Park," my friend B.J.'s husband said. "That's where we go when we camp at Door. It's our favorite park. You'll like it there." I considered B.J. and Dan to be expert campers, so his recommendation carried authority. His words hinted about a lure there, the specifics of which he chose not to describe. I concluded that it would be a personal discovery for both of us once we accepted the richness of the invitation.

Perhaps I had already entered the song of Door the afternoon before. While Loretta was resting, I meditated for the first time in many months. I felt like I had just escaped something that was thwarting my spirit, and now I felt free to be present in my life. I immediately relaxed into the moment of the experience. While meditating, I initially went into a deep state but then returned to a rather light sleep state. As I did that, I heard a message from inside. "Persephone," the voice said. "Persephone, Persephone, Persephone." As I came to full consciousness, I remembered hearing this name before, at a recent lecture I attended regarding mythology. I remembered Persephone was the daughter of some goddess, but that was all I could recall. I wrote down her name, sensing that this was a message I should take very seriously. This kind of thing had never happened to me before, but I was open to listening this weekend. I was willing to hear.

So it was with that kind of awareness that I walked to Newport State Park at Lake Michigan that sunny day in June. The water pulled us to it. We walked along the beach as we approached the wooded area for our hike. I heard the water, felt the water, and entered the essence of that water. Cool, clear lake water. It moved like the ocean, so big and so powerful. Yet it was not the ocean. It was the beauty of fresh water right here in my homeland.

That train of thought led me to a flashback of a very sacred time in my childhood. I remembered the sound of flowing spring water in the creek that ran through the woods where I lived.

I loved that woods, and it became my sanctuary for a number of years. My dog Corky and I spent hours roaming around there. He chased rabbits and I ran after him, believing that maybe someday he would win the chase! It was in those woods that I found a treehouse, which became a sort of home for me. When I needed quiet and comfort, I climbed my treehouse and talked to God. Fall was my favorite time in those woods. I made small leaf houses—another way to create a sense of home, just the way I wanted it.

The lake in front of me whispered to me. "Remember the fall?" it probed. "Remember the crisp Wisconsin air and the wildly dancing trees during the final song of their cycle? Come back. Come and be with us."

We will awaken that song in your heart that has been quiet for so long.

I did remember, and the yearning inside of me gladly accepted the invitation. "Loretta," I said. "I know what I need to do. I have been thinking about taking a vacation by the ocean. But that's not where I need to go. There is nothing I love better than the fall in Wisconsin. I'm coming here—this is where I need to be."

From that moment on, with the decision made, my direction was set. As we talked during that restful, soul-filling weekend, more of the details were worked through. With Persephone as my still unfamiliar guide, I proceeded toward this plan.

The dialogue continued during breakfast on Sunday morning. More pieces fell into place. "I know. I'll talk to the people at Marian College," I told Loretta. "Since I want to go back to school, maybe I can start now. Maybe we can design a way for my fall sabbatical to serve for credit, since it feels like such an important part of my life journey. That's it! Marian is where I need to go." Loretta didn't question any of my ideas that weekend; she simply witnessed the unfolding of a direction she knew was firm.

Later that morning, while Loretta attended to some paperwork, I left to purchase some gifts I had spotted the day before. Also, I wanted to ask people for information regarding a place to stay in the area during September and October. I trusted that I would find what I needed.

I checked with our own resort area before I left. "Good luck," the real estate woman said. "You'll have a hard time finding a place that isn't prohibitively expensive." Somewhat disheartened, I pushed on.

I stopped in Egg Harbor at the studio of Robert Pence. Since he is one of the most established and well-known artists in the area, I thought he might have some helpful information. "Don't know much about that," he said as I asked for his advice. "But there is a real estate company across the street. Try them." It didn't feel like there was a personal connection there. His suggestions just didn't feel like the answer. However, I put the information in my purse, in case I didn't find anything better.

I felt discouraged. Was I asking the impossible? I felt sure I was hearing my inner voice correctly and that something affirming would happen. At this point, my head was leading my inner discussion, and my heart was getting a bit tired.

I continued on to the gift shop in Ephraim. The Red Oak Gift Shop had the gifts that I had seen yesterday. I knew exactly what I wanted, and I quickly chose my gifts. As I approached the counter with multiple purchases, the cashier commented, "You really know what you want, don't you?" We chatted as she began to write up the items. A man came over to help her. I sensed he was the owner, and I asked him about renting a place for the fall.

"I'm in a transition in my life," I said. "I have experienced a lot of changes recently, and I need a place to rest and write for a while."

He responded, "You sound like Jean here." I looked at Jean as she was packaging my purchases and introduced myself. She shared that she was from a small town very near my own home town. We realized that we had met previously just months ago at an open house. I remembered that she was divorced and, as an artist, had recently moved to Door County. I was inspired. What a coincidence. This was a good sign. I had found a connection here!

The energy continued as Doug, her boss, turned his full attention to helping me. He gave me the name of a different rental company along with a very enthusiastic endorsement of their ability to service me. This information boosted my confidence. After picking up Loretta, I headed back home, ready to take the next steps to secure the fall adventure of self-discovery.

Over the next month, the process moved as smoothly as silk. Jill from the Wilson-Shaeffer Real Estate Company became my contact and moved rapidly to fax me available housing options. Although some prices were out of the question, one option looked like it offered everything I needed and at the most reasonable price. This house sat in the woods—just like the house I had lived in as a young girl. A trip back to Door County several weeks later confirmed it. The current renters were happy to show my friend and me through the house. A large table on which to write, a wonderful fireplace, a music system and VCR, a deck facing the morning sun, and a fully-equipped kitchen—all the things I had hoped for. The decision was made at the end of the tour.

I needed to see no more! The contract was signed that day. I headed back to finalize arrangements before heading to my new home in the woods.

The Preparation

I said to my soul, be still, and wait without hope

For hope would be hope for the wrong thing;

   wait without love,

For love would be love of the wrong thing; there is yet faith

But the faith and the love and the hope are all in the waiting.

Wait without thought, for you are not ready for thought:

So the darkness shall be the light,

   and the stillness the dancing.

–T.S. Eliot
"East Coker"
Four Quartets[3]

I was absorbed in trying to understand the mystery.

Persephone? Persephone? Who are you? That was my question; that was my call. In returning home from Door County, I wondered how I would find the answer to that question. I realized that the unfolding of this mystery was bigger than me and that I needed to trust that it would become clear.

First, I wrote one of my friends about the "awakening" of this goddess in my life. When he wrote back, he shared that he too was absorbed in her story. While driving back from his mountain home, prior to picking up the mail with my letter, he had listened to a tape about Persephone and her mother, Demeter. Besides my letter, he received a newsletter entitled "The Mysteries of Life," which focused on Persephone. He sent me both the tape and the newsletter. In addition, my massage therapist gave me a book that she thought would help, *Goddesses in Everywoman*, which recounted the entire story of Persephone as the "Maiden and Queen of the Underworld."[4] To augment that, I found references in several books in my own library. Persephone began to unfold as the spiritual partner who would hold my hand as I entered my own underworld of self-discovery and healing.

In early August, as I was leaving my massage therapist, I noticed a brochure on the table entitled "Mandala, The Goddess Within." Reading it, I discovered an invitation to a workshop that explored the evolution of our goddess within through art and meditation. It was scheduled for the weekend before my departure to Door County. It was the ritual of preparation I needed. I registered immediately.

It was intriguing to me, as I entered the retreat grounds, that this lovely center was located so close to my home. I didn't know any of the women, however, who had chosen to attend, and I felt a bit anxious as I arrived.

Twenty women decided to spend their weekend in this artistic process. Some of them were related. There was Ann and her daughter, who acted very much alike. Mimi and her daughter were quite the opposite of each other. Carol, who arrived the next day, shared that she just lost her job. Chris told us how nervous she was about her lack of artistic skill (which gave me great relief!), even though she had been at this retreat before. Our facilitator, Willow, was joined by her mother and sister. Most people knew each other from previous gatherings. I was a newcomer.

With great trepidation, I entered the process. "Too late now," I thought as I simply surrendered to whatever would be. "I am what I am—I am not what I am not. I need to trust, and something will happen." But the discomfort I felt in spite of those rational thoughts remained for the first several hours.

After a meditation (which initiated each session throughout the weekend), Willow offered some tools to help us. We started with some basic shading exercises—white pencil on black paper. It looked easy enough, so I began. When Willow stopped at my place to give support, she showed me how I could loosen up and let the pencil lead me, and the pencil and I reached an understanding of each of our roles.

We worked with white on black the rest of Friday evening. By Saturday morning, we were ready to begin our goddess mandala on a larger black sheet that each of us had been given. Mandalas are simply circular images representing the universe in Hindu and Buddhist symbolism. Creating mandalas helps us recommit to claiming our own strengths, authenticity, and purpose. First, Willow instructed, we were to develop the image from within using only the white pencil. Color would be introduced later.

I was petrified. Creating the circle was easy, but it sat staring at me, almost daring me to go ahead. All my negative internal messages came forward. By now I knew that most of the people in the room were what I would call "official artists." What was I doing here? How humiliating! Again, I remembered that I am who I am. "Just be still, and walk," my inner voice told me. So I did. I walked right over to the plastic forms in the middle of the floor there to help us in case we needed them. I chose circles and triangles as something to get me started.

I drew circles going all the way into the center of my mandala. Then I drew some triangles on each side, going outward. "Quite the geometrical form," I thought. I wondered how what I was doing related to the image of a goddess. Where, oh where, was Persephone?

I don't remember all the details except that we worked in about two-hour increments. In each meditation before we began, I asked with all my heart that the image inside of me express itself. Sometimes I saw images or colors, and then I took them to the paper. Every session ended with what we called a "walk around." We put our drawings on the floor in front of us, forming a circle. Then we walked around, stopping at each image in front of us to meditate on it and experience the giving and receiving of energy between us and the drawing. Each drawing was symbolic of the transformation of our group as we became more and more connected.

When I began coloring the core circle of the mandala, I realized that my drawing had life. I felt its heartbeat and soul beat as I watched the intensity of the golds, yellows, and reds working together to create the power in the center of the mandala. The radiance going out in all directions began to form her body, and the symbols around her represented her life energy. By Sunday morning, there she was: Persephone in all her aura! Earth, air, fire, and water surrounded her. The undulating circles gave her the option to go down under or to come back up, revealing her availability to journey with me as I entered the underworld of solitude.

By Sunday afternoon, she was completely out of me. I stood proudly next to the other artists; I was one too! I now defined "artist" as one who allows an image to come through her, something we all did. Some drawings were more aesthetically beautiful than others, but each one was intense and profound. All of the goddesses together in the final walk around filled us with shared energy. With all of the goddesses fully emerged, the beauty was in the whole, consisting of all the parts. All of us were an integral part of a larger drawing of life energy. This energy welled up in me as I left, Persephone in hand, to embark on my journey to the woods.

The Journey Home

I prepare myself to meet her
Knowing not what to say
It has not been only men
who have betrayed her
I have betrayed her as well

I have been a father's daughter
rejecting my mother
I have always been afraid of
moving down into the darkness
I might lose
consciousness

I might lose
my voice
my vision
my equilibrium

How much of it is really mine?
My words are encased in others'
language
My images are derivative of
others' art
What *is* me?

–Maureen Murdock
"*Looking for the Lost Pieces of Myself*"
The Heroine's Journey:
Woman's Quest for Wholeness[5]

The time for my transition and healing had come.

The alarm rang at 5:00 a.m. The plan was to be packed and on my way to Door County by 8:00. There was a restlessness in my stomach. I had procrastinated until there was no time left to procrastinate. It was time to begin the journey. It was, in fact, Monday, September 2nd — Labor Day!

As I prepared to leave one home, I packed things that would make the house in the woods my new home. I took the gifts good friends had given me just days before: the turtle pin to remind me to go slowly, the lovely angel ornament to remind me of all the angels I have at home, and a special book and stuffed rabbit from a dear friend I call my sister to remind me of her deep caring and concern.

Additionally, I packed pictures of my children and good friends, candles, plants, cookbooks, and about fifty of my favorite books. And, of course, Persephone, who was still in the car from the weekend. With my car full of the mirrors of my soul and my bike finally securely fastened to the outside, I was ready to begin the journey.

At 8:00 a.m., just as planned, I left my house. Labor Day already had become real to me. I had "labored" hard since early morning to prepare for the trip. Now as I drove out of town, I began to think about the larger connection. This drive felt like being "in labor." It was uncomfortable. I sat in the unknown space of expectation—not knowing whether I was giving birth or being birthed, I felt both the pain and the joy of this transition. All I knew for sure was that I was beginning an experience that would change my life, and I could not turn back.

The trip went smoothly. I arrived at the real estate office around 11:00, picked up my keys, and headed to the little cabin, just a mile and a half outside of a small town named Fish Creek. As I drove in the driveway, I felt like a foreigner arriving in a new country. "Hello, woods! Hello, house! Hello, self! I have arrived!"

I felt no sense of rejection; I heard only the silence. My presence was not in violation of whatever was going on here. The woods accepted my arrival. I opened the door and began to make a new home for myself in the house in the woods.

After two hours of unpacking and rearranging, I sat down and listened to some music. It felt like I belonged here. Just the trees and me, like when I was young, sitting in my treehouse. We had so much to talk about, to cry about, to remember. I remembered the feeling and the sound of the trees back then. Was that the voice of my God? I knew, really knew, that I was home again, where God and the trees could heal all those years since we had last been together. I looked up at Persephone, whose image I had taped high up on the inside of the deck door, and wondered whether I had the courage to go where she was taking me.

Later, as I began to write, I reflected:

> *Persephone will take me through the darkness, but she tells me to remember that her center is the brightest light imaginable. It sustains her. It is fiery red – the fire of life. Through all deaths, the essence survives. Not to be afraid. She looks so complete. She has so much of the experience of life in her. She is full, strong, and fluid in her energy. She will walk with me, and she will be there for me. We have places to go I don't know about. She mesmerizes me at night. What is she trying to say? Where does she want me to go?*

Thus began the process of emptying and remembering, remembering and emptying, that took me into the depths of my being. I chose to start by fasting, a literal emptying of my physical self. Fresh fruit and vegetable juices sustained me for three days. On the third day, I wrote, "I can feel the layers of my insides peeling away. There is so much memory there—so much pain."

The discomfort of the depths soothed itself in interesting ways. Ritual and routine became the structure that held me together. Each day I would design a new daily pattern, always looking for the one that was just right. Once I got it, the fun was in the rebellion of challenging it and redoing it the very next day. For example, sometimes I would make my juice first, then write, then do a reflective tape, then walk, and then swim. The next day I would make my juice, listen to the tape, write, swim, and then walk. This might seem confusing, but it was rather comical. I accepted the game as a way to lighten the heaviness of the place I was in.

Reflection was always an important part of each morning. Initially I listened to a tape series called "Days of Renewal,"[6] by Fr. Richard Rohr. As time went on, the concept of "renewal" became more descriptive of my transition. The tapes led me to think about my relationship with myself and God. Just two days after arriving, I wrote:

I am more and more sure that I was meant to understand the beauty and deep meaning of the human experience. Sometimes I think it is the work I must do for my family. Sometime along the way, perhaps many lifetimes ago, my family shut down its feelings. The injury was so deep. Methods of numbing were used by its members, and control became the method of survival. Strength became defined as outsmarting the other one, never becoming so vulnerable that someone could stomp you out. Women were particularly hurt by this. They had no way to be of value. They were supposed to be the joy and the hope, always finding fun and energy. They had to be strong and beautiful.

Other than that, their job was to have the family, raise the family, be there for the husband, and not cause too much trouble.

But this inability to feel, this inability developing from years of repression, caused such gaps for me. Where was this Jesus I read about? Where was this Love I could trust? Where was anything I could trust? What I hear is that becoming vulnerable, trying to be open to loving and becoming – sometimes failing miserably – sometimes feeling abandoned and completely empty – that THIS is the human experience.

Right now, my mind is full and crazy with everything at once. I so want to make linear sense of it, but I must be with the complexity of it. I may have to be with the pieces and then see how they fit into a labyrinth of life color. My questions remain. Who am I as a woman, as mother, as partner, as daughter, as sister, as human, as godliness?

During those first few days, I read my journals from the past several years. That caused me to go back further, always back to my time in the woods as a young girl. I wrote:

It is the time to accept a trance with the trees and remember back when I was young with my dog. I remember sitting in that treehouse and wondering about God and who would love me. Where would I go, and why was I born? As I remember, I held my inner pain out to that soft breeze I felt up there. The smell of the trees through the seasons, the running stream, the rabbits – all these memories seemed connected with my remembering God.

Remembering the time in the treehouse sparked memories of my mother. During that time, she encountered a life-changing illness that resulted in the removal of three quarters of her stomach. My father and brothers did not share with either my mother or me that the ulcer removed during that surgery was cancerous. My notes go on:

I remember my mother. Just for a second I allow myself to remember what it was like to be with her without the fear of her dying. We were great friends. She was who I trusted. Then she got sick, and everything changed.

Perhaps that is when that inner pain began.

During this time of reflection about the past, I was brought back to the present remembering a conversation with my first husband, Nick, and his fiancée, Anna. They were uncomfortable with their quickly approaching wedding plans. They wanted to be married in the Catholic Church. That required annulments of both of their marriages. I supported this decision, since I did not want to create a block to the marriage. However, it renewed an old wound inside, and I found myself faced with the need for some healing I hadn't expected.

"We need to renew our relationship," Nick said. "It is different now than when we were married." We agreed that we would always care about each other. The annulment gave us the opportunity to let go of the past and reclaim our friendship in the present. I thought I was here in the woods to heal the loss of my second marriage which had ended just eight months ago. But there I was, back to the heart of my first marriage that had ended in divorce almost twelve years ago. Part of me cried inside, even after all these years. Renewal sounded nice but didn't feel very good. I realized that the child in me was crying but wasn't lost. She had been coming to this place in stages and longed to grow. I knew the mother part of me needed to hold her and comfort her. Then she would be ready to move on.

I found myself reflecting through listening to old music: Joan Baez, Ian and Sylvia, and Judy Collins. The songs brought back memories of my college years. I felt the sting of loneliness, something I had felt back then. I remembered how Nick and I moved into a serious relationship during those years. The ache inside expressed itself:

> *I know I am not fully embraced in my imperfection by a partner, as I have always longed to be. I wonder how much of that is a yearning for a mother's love — the safety of being held by mother. I wonder if I am going to pass through the waters of that yearning to my womanhood. I feel such a need to totally yield to my own roots, to my own sense of existence.*

I processed through a myriad of memories during those first two weeks. At midday, I found relief by heading to Peninsula State Park, where I found a small beach. The temperature hovered around seventy degrees, so I was able to swim. The water was so cold. It was a struggle to overcome my resistance to get in the water, but once I did, I found it comforting and refreshing. Just lying in the sun after the swim, resting and thinking about nothing, I sustained my spirit while I lived in the depths of my life review.

Remembering, experiencing the pain, and then letting go — my mother, my marriages, my children, my work, my dreams. I even had to let go of Persephone. While attending a weekend seminar during this period, I left the drawing, rolled in a mailing tube, in a rental car. This loss presented new pain in addition to experiencing the old. I felt empty.

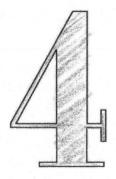

Going Deeper

Life is about Listening
to the wind blowing in the fall,
to the music as each note trails off,
to the song of the bird on our walk,
to the person desperately needing to be heard.

Life is about Seeing
the bright pink orchid in the woods
when it isn't supposed to be there,
the green caterpillar that would be missed for a leaf,
the spider web so carefully woven in the trees,
the lonely look on the face of the person you just passed.

Life is about Touching
the rock among rocks that calls you,
the huge tree in the middle of the forest

recording so many years,
the life-filled fur of a dog,
the hand of a person filled with the pain of life.

Life is about Feeling
the cool fall air that demands deepening,
the privilege of the healing touch of massage,
the excruciating pain before rushes of tears finally come,
the love of another human being from a heart that has no choice.

Yes, Life is about Listening
to the silence that is filled with the sound of truth.

—Virginia Duncan Gilmore
"Life Is about Listening"
HJ Personal Journal[7]

My senses felt the oncoming unrest and transformation.

After a little more than two weeks of reviewing my life and touching the pain of some major changes and losses, the experience began to intensify. When I read the first chapter of *The Artist's Way*,[8] I decided to follow the recommendation of the author, Julia Cameron, and write three pages of free thoughts each morning. These entries are referred to by Cameron as "morning pages."[9] Prior to this, I had been typing reflections every couple of days, which I decided to continue as well. My journal was large, allowing me ample space to ramble. Realizing I would be writing every day made me more sensitive and aware to what was happening to me, both during the day and at night. I honored this commitment for the rest of my stay in Door County, and the journal contains a rich and full accounting of my experience.

On September 19, the first day of the journal entry, my writing had a tone of confusion. For the first time I talked about the experience of "opening," which became a major metaphor during the next couple of weeks. "I seem to be opening up—getting less and less afraid." I longed for my truth. I felt the need to let go, mostly of the people I had been hanging onto. I particularly recalled my two marriages.

For the first time, I began to really notice the outdoors. The more internally focused I became, the more sensitive I became to the world outside my little house. I remembered what brought me to the woods. "What a beautiful day," I wrote. "The sky is potent blue against the still-green trees." Perhaps I was sensing the oncoming change of the season. Perhaps I was sensing unrest in the woods as it prepared to transform and let go. Perhaps we were beginning to feel the harmony of each other's presence.

I felt drawn to deal with my feelings about losing the mandala drawing—Persephone. She had carried me to the depths of my inner self. I described her in my journal:

She was so vital, so intense. It was hard for me to look at her, but I did, and she infused her image and her colors on my brain. She is lost in one form but kept always in my mind and in my heart. Somehow she is telling me something. I hear her telling me to heal my heart. "Let the healing continue. Do not sidetrack." She tells me to remember my power, my inner glow.

However, she also warns me to remember the red spots, the still bleeding spots. "Healing takes time; healing comes, oh, so slowly." With healing happening each day, I feel some new life. Sometimes I feel so utterly abandoned, but at least I am not abandoning myself!

Those feelings of abandonment brought forth more memories of my mother. She died when I was twenty-five, after her third round with cancer. For many years, I felt a hole in my heart because she had never said goodbye to me, never said she loved me as she died, and left me no letters. Even though I knew that the culture at that time did not encourage open discussion of the dying process, that did not heal the painful void. Yet I was thankful for the gifts my mother had given me. At a weekend program I was attending called "Mystery School," through a shaman exercise in which we shared unhealed areas in our souls with a partner, I reconnected with the spirit of my mother. My partner, acting as shaman, served as the vessel through which she spoke. After learning that my mother had suffered a laryngectomy, he acted out receiving her larynx in his own body. Now, with my mother's voice inside him, the words just came out. "I love you, Ginny. I love you, Ginny. I love you, Ginny." I will never forget those words and the healing power they gave me. I knew she was released as well by having a channel to give this significant message to her daughter.

My inner child believed those words. The rest of me felt happy for that child. I wanted to take better care of her, and, for that matter, the rest of me too. It was the beginning of a bridge from that deep sense of abandonment back to myself. In my final words of the very first "morning page" entry, I wrote:

The left side of my back hurts. Perhaps it is about the blocks to my creativity that get all clustered in my body: my fears about abandonment, rejection, etc., in relationship to creativity emerging. I really feel I'm on to something. My body wants to dance. Well, lots of me wants to dance. My heart is big and vibrant and

accessible. Some will accept my invitation; others will be too
afraid. That's okay. I like it. I like my heart. I like "being" from it.
That is where I want to stay!

During this time I started spending time with Jean, the artist
friend who had helped me find the house in Door County. I got a
bit nervous about how deep I was getting and needed someone to
talk to about it. Jean and I began sharing regular walks in the
woods. Our first walk lasted several hours. We slowly moved
through a sanctuary that held more mystery than any other
woods I'd seen. Jean, in her artist's way, noticed things I didn't. I
realized how I had moved through life "seeing" very little. At one
point, we stopped to listen. In the quietness, there were many
sounds that we had missed earlier. The rich life energy of this
wooded space taught us how to truly "know" it.

This experience stayed with me, and an inner voice spoke to
me early the next morning. A poem flowed out of me. "Life Is
about Listening" was written in the second day of my journal.

With sharpening awareness, I began to trust this alone experience.

I truly love this time. It is so rich. It is so real. I am learning to
know what I really like. I continue to write about people in my life
who have hurt me, but the language softens. Movement toward
self-acceptance and self-forgiveness is evolving. By last night I
was really comfortable being on my own with my God. It has been
so long since I felt I could try to look straight at my God, and I am
doing that now. I think I feel the heart of God often. It is there for
me, and I know I truly want to serve that Love with my life.

During this time of rapid learning and remembering, I started to consider how to keep the solitude and peace I had found. I worried about the future and was reminded of what I didn't like about the life I had left behind. "Being too busy is what I don't like. This quiet time feels pretty wonderful to me for now." I began to recognize that this experience was limited, and I needed to embrace it as deeply as I could. I made a commitment to myself to keep searching for what I enjoyed most and to incorporate that into my life.

Then I realized how much I missed my children. Like the limited time I had for this sabbatical, I became aware of the limited time I had with my children at this stage in their lives. I thought about how their lives will change once they are out of school and settled. I considered the probability of my own life changing as I move more toward my purpose. I decided to spend as much time as possible with them. Perhaps it was that internal voice again showing me what I enjoy. "I enjoy my children," I confirmed. I began to envision all of us spending a wonderful Thanksgiving together. It seemed vital. As this vision grew over the next several days, I started planning for both children to be home for the holiday. Thoughts were coming on all levels. I remembered the past; I became more sensitive to the present; and I began to imagine the future. At the same time, I felt real pain along with forgiveness and surrender. The joy of the gift I was giving myself was mixed with the anxiety of the coming changing season, for the trees and for myself. Nothing was simple during this period. It was complex. I wrote:

> *I sit in the same living area, day after day, looking out at the same trees, each one so different yet the scene is so much the same. I see a leaf fall, as many do right now, as the season finally gives in to change. Some fall, and some remain, only to begin to die in their beautiful, radiant yellow, orange, or red color. The expectation of death and color is in the gray sky and the rather non-distinct air today.*

With the multiple layers I was experiencing, I began to create more structure in my day. I became convinced that discipline would serve me well. "Isn't it discipline that makes someone really strong?" I wrote the following response:

> *I now write each day in my "morning pages." Interesting thoughts flow out from either the day before or the adventurous night. Then I fix my juice. Quite the ritual that is — I must peel the orange, wash the peach, wash the grapes, and then cut them all up for the juicer to change their form. It doesn't take very long, and I have the pristine juice to pour into the elegant wine glass.*

> *There it stands, all ready for me. But I put it aside to protect it from spilling while I wash the dishes and the juicer parts. Then I clean up the peel, and finally I am ready for my juice. At this point I have some gentle music on, and I sit in the deck chair I bought earlier, which has been moved inside. I sit there, generally thinking of something that makes me nervous and drinking my juice too quickly! It is wonderful, though, as I always remember that the juice is very healthy. The juice is the first thing that*

enters my system after the array of ten blue-green algae pills that I have taken earlier. Then I go to get dressed for the big hike. I get my book on tape, which always goes into the top left pocket of my Amazon Smythe shirt. I grab my three stones, which were finally selected as the personalized method of measurement of my walk, and off I go. I walk first to my left, up the hill. I walk six times around, then change direction and walk six times the other way. The three stones have been exchanged four times, and the three miles are complete.

Ironically, after all that, I write:

I don't have much of this glorious time here left. How I love it – just getting away from all the detail of the busyness at home. I love the simplicity of it. I love the special creativity of my own design. I love the quiet of it. I love all this time with God. It is exquisite indeed, and it has a limit to it I see!

Toward the end of the entry, I got closer to my innermost core:

Oh, the quiet. Sometimes it is so empty and so incredibly lonely. I feel so utterly alone, and then I remember that I chose to be here. I want to know the God so many write about as they move through the veil that has been clouding their access. How long will it take? Can I do it? Will God be there for me? Of course God is there for me, I answer, but wonder if I really believe it. I know I am safe. I feel a Love around me that I don't have words to describe. I don't want that to end. I don't want to leave. What is ahead for me now? How can I stay with this sense of peacefulness and choice?

I thought often about Persephone. I wanted to try to draw her again. I had bought paper but didn't risk drawing her until much later. I remembered the spiral image that I drew on the bottom left corner—a symbol of the wind. Spirals were coming up often in my other drawings, and had for quite some time. As I thought about it, I recalled that I drew spirals from the inside out.

I began to compare the image of the opening spiral to myself:

I feel like I have been so tightly closed. And now, little by little, I am opening. It takes time; it takes trust in my God. I need to expand my sense of existence, my consciousness, to be much bigger than just my life and what is in it. My life seems like crisp, clear, spring water, running down the canyon. Perhaps I want it to feel more like the ocean. My memory is better now. I think I am giving it permission to remember at times. Uncoiling is freeing it up to remember.

Again, as I allowed this time of opening, I needed to get in touch with ritual. I found myself at a Catholic church for Sunday Mass. I was deeply moved by the death and resurrection of Jesus and his offering of Himself to each of us. To be in communion with my God and the church community was especially meaningful to me during this inner turmoil and deep searching. I wrote further:

It seems that as I open or uncoil from all the resistance inside me, I want to go further with my self-disclosure and self-discussion. I began to accept the love of my God in my deep pain and aloneness. As I accepted that Love, I recognized that I knew Love. I truly love my children. Many people dear to me have disappointed me or hurt me. I still love them. I must accept them as they are. In that love, I feel the sense of forgiveness. I am learning that in loving myself. I am beginning to forgive myself. As I do that, feeling the love of my God helping me to open to this, I begin to extend this same love and forgiveness to others. Forgiveness opens the door for acceptance of the other person on his or her terms, not mine, and that seems so important to surrendering to love.

Nothing occurred in a linear fashion. As I focused on loving and forgiving myself, I could feel this overflowing to my relationship with others. I felt full and yet empty, connected and alone— all at the same time. One day I came home from a walk and journaled:

I'm not so sure I like this new role of a single, fifty-year-old woman, divorced twice. But that's who I am! It is important to continue to open my heart to my own forgiveness. Some of us act out our dark sides and then make peace with it; perhaps others repress it or dress it up in something that looks virtuous. But we all have it. I must learn how to forgive and surrender to the acceptance. I have more questions today than answers. Surrender is the word on which I want to focus. It seems like I need to do that, but I resist. I am taught to be such a survivor. I think I need to realize that the life flow has ebbs and tides, and none of us flows in perfect harmony all the time. But there will be moments of it. One day at a time.

Then came a breakthrough. After falling asleep early one evening, I awoke to watch a television show about a young couple meeting in Europe. Something about the way their relationship developed touched my heart. I sat and cried. I felt something happening to me. I could feel myself open and receive the Grace I needed. Before I left home, I had started a small book of words that now held special meaning for me. I had brought the book with me, but up until this time, no new words had been added. I added four important words that night: vessel, opening, grace, and legitimate. Somehow it all made sense. I wasn't angry anymore. I understood:

It seems that this time is about the willingness to let go. It isn't about finding the answers or the love, except for the Love in the Grace that comes when I open to it. I have been so coiled for so long, and opening my heart is long, tedious, and sometimes painful work. If I don't grieve, I can't feel and heal. I am grieving. I am being asked to accept many losses or changes right now. When I feel God's grace, I feel safe. I feel at home. I feel loved. But it is up to me to do the opening – to be willing to let go and trust.

The quiet time is absolutely essential for that. I must have it. I can now arrange my life for that. If I can learn to be present, then each day is as big as a lifetime. I want to live it, to see as much as possible every moment and to stay open to the energy of life, deeply painful and huge in its joy!

As the month of September drew to an end, it became clear what was happening. I knew I was "home" again:

This place feels more like what I lost than anything. My place in the woods when I was young was personal and precious to me. I made it safe for myself. I went up in that treehouse and connected with my God. This, here, is a small version of that spiritual connection. My fears are beginning to get challenged, and I am moving through them. I am beginning to accept this new role of being fifty and alone. My resistance is finally cracking. I am emerging to make friends with it. The Grace periods are what I love the most. Like right now. I feel the Grace coming to me as I surrender the old and open to the new. The Universe is listening. I can tell.

The Fall

Sabbaths 1979, I

I go among trees and sit still.
All my stirring becomes quiet
around me like circles on water.
My tasks lie in their places
where I left them, asleep like cattle.

Then what is afraid of me comes
and lives a while in its sight.
What it fears in me leaves me,
and the fear of me leaves it.
It sings, and I hear its song.

Then what I am afraid of comes.
I live for a while in its sight.

What I fear in it leaves it,
and the fear of it leaves me.
It sings, and I hear its song.

After days of labor,
mute in my consternations,
I hear my song at last,
and I sing it. As we sing,
the day turns, the trees move.

—Wendell Berry
This Day: Collected &
New Sabbath Poems[10]

I was awakening to the newness and the greatest sense of being.

I was midway through my sabbatical in Door County. As I approached October 1st, my tension grew. Engaging in the second half of the experience seemed important and necessary. It reminded me of other big changes in my life, like when my first child left for college. It seemed like I prepared for it a year ahead. When the actual transition came, I was ready and almost grateful that it was finally happening. The final days leading to October 1st were filled with the same kind of trepidation. I felt a sort of relief and sense of newness as I moved into this second phase.

I was drawn to a book in the local bookstore titled *Woman: Image of the Holy Spirit*. The book intrigued me and met my needs as I continued to ask questions about God. In her book, Joan Schaupp shares a thought that flashed into her mind while praying during communion: "I'm made in the image of God, but I'm really not like God, the Father. Nor am I an exact image of Christ. . . . Then who am I like? I must be an image of the Holy Spirit . . . for the Spirit is love, gives birth."[11] Joan proceeds to share the in-depth research showing biblical references that convince her that woman is in the image of the Holy Spirit.[12] In addition, she talks about Mary as the "image of the eternal feminine." She continues, "In some manner, Mary is related to all the feminine imagery associated with the Holy Spirit: 'Tent of Yahweh, Seat of Wisdom, Glory of God.' The Second Vatican Council recognized this symbolic relationship between Mary and the Holy Spirit, perhaps unconsciously, calling Mary 'Advocate,' 'Helper.'"[13] This awakening of my spirit brought new energy to my days. The Spirit became a friend, and in a way, another name for the energy I saw in Persephone. The spirals on the mandala symbolizing wind spoke to me of the Holy Spirit. I could still see the resiliency of the colors and light moving through them. I felt the movement of this new Energy helping me to uncoil, opening up to the fullness of the human experience. Renewing my relationship with Mary was also very joyful for me. Mary had always been a part of my life. People with the gift of seeing auras or channeling told me more than once that Mary was walking with me. I understood the connection and felt a Grace of understanding that stayed with me throughout the rest of my stay.

I became more aware of being filled with joy. Often I wrote about this as I faced the choices about my future. The recent ending of my marriage as well as a seventeen-year career left some big gaps for me. These endings opened the door for new possibilities. "I get better each week. I am more ready to accept my role in life. I know I can do this, and I have lots of joy. The freedom and choice are unbelievable!"

However, I go on to write about the fact that I have no partner now. Regularly in my journal entries, I struggle with this void in my life and my desire to know love. I feel the emptiness of not having anyone to hold me, to plan with me. I fluctuate between this longing for connection and relationship and my fullness of the Grace of God. I feel empty and full at the same time. In the fullness of fall, the trees seem to soothe my confusion and frustration.

The changes of the forest each day, the transformation of the trees, filled me with images and thoughts:

The colors are coming, more every day. I watch the leaves crescendo their beauty, only then to let go and fall to the ground. What an experience to watch and feel! Do they know what they are facing? Or are the leaves shocked when, in their greatest glory, they suddenly feel the tree letting go of them? Or do they let go of the tree? Isn't that what it is all about – to know the rhythm of life and to get in synchronicity with it, flowing with it in great splendor and simple acceptance? What do the leaves tell me about surrender, acceptance, and forgiveness? Some are holding onto the tree in all its majesty and will fall without ever knowing the color. Some turn very quickly at the first opportunity and are down early before the moment of peak grandeur when the symphony of color reaches its radiance of diversified richness: yellow, orange, red, gold, brown.

It's that pristine moment when the forest says "ah, yes!" This is the jeweled moment, that moment of the greatest sense of being. This is the crystallized moment of the celebration of the end and the time just before the letting go into the death and tunnel of hibernation, or the tomb, or "the change" — to be later reborn, resurrected, renewed — to enter once again the process of becoming.

The trees with their story and costume of leaves show us the process each year. But we, through our multiple deaths and rebirths, experience the costume or design of our lives over a long, long period. What are the trees telling me? To go slowly, I think. Not always to be first so as to miss the peak of the greatness. I am learning the sowing, the waiting, the surrender, and acceptance. Let it happen. Let the contents of my being just move at their pace. Let the colors emerge. Try different ways to make colors, to learn different ways, to open the creative heart energy, to open all the valves of energy!

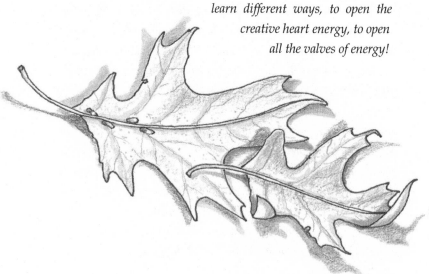

After energy-filled and grace-filled days such as the one in which this imagery poured forth, I noticed that I would experience a letdown the next day. When this happened more than once, I mentioned it to my massage therapist. She gently suggested that I remember to stay grounded as I moved into higher levels of consciousness. In fact, she felt the tension worsening in my back after one of the higher consciousness days. After an hour and a half mostly spent on loosening this area, I was convinced that I needed to heed her advice during times of unfolding spiritual awareness. I remembered to stay centered, to let go of what wasn't mine, drink lots of water, and get lots of rest. This helped as new spiritual consciousness happened more often, and the joy remained.

Prayer and meditation were increasingly inviting me. Meditation was difficult for me as I found myself busy taking walks, answering messages, reading, and listening to tapes. However, it came to me, again through the trees!

One sunny morning, while on my way back from the post office, I stopped to see the ducks in the water at a small beach in Fish Creek. Sitting there, I looked up to the left and noticed a grapevine climbing up a tree whose branches bore still-green leaves. However, the vine had moved into its grand fall melody with an intensity of color that captured my attention and mesmerized me. The Spirit wanted to talk to me for a while:

The vine had turned such a strong red I could hardly look. But I did look. It was a fire, it was love, it was power beyond understanding, and it reminded me again of how big God is. That red – that vibrant, intense, burning red – is what is inside of me, ready to be. It is so bright that it makes its way through all the

*layers of protection I put over it. People respond to it, even in very
dim doses. I want, more and more, to be with this red sense of
eternity in me, to tear away the shrouds over it so it can shine
through. Indeed, we are all channels for the all-powerful God. This
red reveals the elements of God to me. It has the light and the dark,
the gentle and the powerful, the softness and intensity, the life and
death, the heart and blood, and the Life, Hope, and Love of the
Holy Spirit, the Breath of God.*

Later I write, "It is the woundedness and the healing.
Persephone showed that in her picture. I want to draw again, but
I am afraid. I feel the healing, but not without tugs and pulls of
resistance and anxiety." Even with all the inspiration, my human-
ness hung on, going in and out of pure ecstasy and deep fear.

An example of the spectrum of my emotions comes through in
the morning pages:

*What is the pain I feel? It stretches my being in utter loneliness. It
fills my cells with light and dark at the same time. Who am I?
I am happy here. It dances here. The panoramic symphony of color
just giggles with its sense of itself! It knows this is the greatest of
its performances, and yet it keeps tickling us like the trickster as
if to say:*

*"Keep looking — maybe you will see the majesty of the most
precious gift in us. But we'll divert you; we will, indeed. We have
many tunes within the opera, each of them with its own rhythm.
Each wants your attention. There are many of us in this
community of Fallness. As we fall — the I in We-ness of it all — we
call out in our peak of golden red to notice the one moment of
our radiant perfection. 'Look here — no, look over here,' we all*

scream out. We look and look and get caught up in their celebration of creativity. Our quickly turning heads feel the laughter of the play."

As one tree becomes barren of the splendor, another moves into soprano ecstasy with its vibration into the beginning of the end. Many miraculous moments, and then the sound of the music falls softer to the darkness of the colder days.

The fall kept beckoning me, and I walked more and more. The lure of the forest entranced me, and I wanted to stay there forever. As I heard the beat of the leaves' song, I felt the "rhythm of my own creation." I felt safe—so content. Occasionally, I needed to go back to my permanent home, just for a day. I didn't find any connection to it, and I wondered if it would ever feel like "home" again.

I began the bargaining process with myself to find a way to stay in the blissful state of responsibility only to myself and my woods in Door. Over and over, I tried to justify staying, but it just didn't come. Deep inside I could feel the pull back to the community I had left behind. A new sense of energy permeated me. I found myself rising earlier and thinking about what I would do and who I would be when I returned:

Right now, I am interested to have as much exposure to writing and culture that I can so as to stretch myself. I want to better serve. I am believing more and more that the Universe wants me on the team, and I have a legitimate role to play. Now I need more energy and discipline and a willingness to work hard toward my becoming.

It is participating in the circle of life that is so complete and renewing!

As the trees and their transformation intensified, so too did my gratitude and my connectedness to their story. I feel moved to enter my thoughts into the journal:

There is so much energy right now to the peaking crescendo. For just a moment, it is complete, and then the Fall begins. The energy is too great — the song of life took all these leaves had, something like the Song of Jesus. Then they are finished; it is done. They let go and fall to the ground, where they join the floor community of the forest to go back to a different form, providing food for the continuation process. The stable trunk, which gave the leaves arms with which to connect, is in mourning. All the aliveness of the family has let go. The leaves now find a way to feed all those trunks and the essence of potential radiance again and again. The leaves feel so familiar — so approachable, but the trunks feel more formal. Is that because they reflect the knowing, the wisdom of the cycles of life?

Perhaps that is what we need to remember. The Universe provides the nourishment, or the trunk, for us to live a full life of green. Then, at the peak, we reflect the multiple colors of the great Love within us. Yes, the cycle of life has a beginning, a radiant peak, and an ending of sorts, but the ending always nourishes the beginning. It is the circle that holds the richness. It is participating in the circle of life that is so complete and renewing. What are the woods helping me to remember? It is the knowing of those trunks that gives me courage and hope. They know God, they reflect the Big Story, and they seem to love me.

I began walking regularly at sunset. I planted myself in a good spot to watch the colors in the sky appear as the sun fell into the water. This exercise seemed appropriate. As the trees were nearing the sunset of their season, I, too, was approaching the sunset of my Door County time.

Again, I experienced more life reviews. I continued to reflect on my relationship with my mother. I believed our relationship held so many pearls to the mystery of my life. As I reviewed her life, I realized that I had made different decisions than she had. I had choices, and I was taking the risk to live my life. I missed her, and I hoped I had her blessing as I began to turn the corner toward the final two weeks of my journey.

Reflection

In the Bible, when someone touches Christ,

he or she is healed.

It is not just touching a cloth

that brings about a miracle.

When you touch deep understanding and love,

you are healed.

—Thich Nhat Hanh
Living Buddha, Living Christ[14]

The tension inside my body grew!

As I approached the last two weeks, I was so afraid of losing what I had found during this precious time in my life. Repeatedly, I reminded myself of what I had learned here. Changes would be necessary to maintain the quiet time. Priorities needed to be identified and honored. I particularly missed my children during my time in the woods, and I determined to love them even more than I had. To spend more time with them, listening to them and honoring them, being as present to them as possible. "I don't want my calendar to run my life like it did," I wrote. Yet, I struggled with the fear that I would somehow forget and lose what I had gained.

This fear came to a climax on a Wednesday in mid-October. My massage therapist again confirmed that tension was showing up in my body. I was ruffled when I left—quite dissatisfied that I hadn't learned the art of relaxation yet. Consequently, I immediately headed to my favorite woods at Newport Park, the same state park where I initially heard "the call" to come to Door County.

It was a beautiful day, about seventy degrees. The sky was clear blue, and fall was in full bloom. I walked quite a distance, maybe two miles or so. I wandered toward the private lake that my friend Jean and I had discovered days earlier. It was like discovering heaven:

> *I felt like I owned this lake. You have never seen such beautiful weather. It was warm enough to take my shoes off and walk in the water. I sat with my feet in the water and wrote a letter. I read a bit. It was so peaceful. This was as close to Nirvana as I have come. I was totally at one and at peace. I felt connected to the Universe. I felt filled and not lonely. I will always remember this time here, when I emptied out my busyness and opened myself to nature.*

Even so, I continued to be restless, yet I received what I needed. One night, I woke up at 2:30 a.m. and experienced a small anxiety attack. I felt led to read and grabbed a magazine called *Lotus, Personal Transformation*. I read many of the articles, but one of them seemed to tie together so much of what I was learning. In "The Seat of Prosperity," Rick Jarow talks about living from the heart. In summary, he states:

> *The basic principle of working with the heart chakra is to create a palpable circuit of giving and receiving. . . . Letting go of a preconceived outcome, our destiny appears. . . . As the spasm of non-alignment subsides and the intellect settles in its rightful place, we can move more easily with our heart's desire. Rebirth means living the life of the heart.*[15]

I was inspired enough to get my word journal and add the words "acceptance" and "alignment." Then peace came and I fell asleep easily.

Yet the erratic emotional swings kept coming. One moment I was filled with joy, and the next I was in tears. I underwent the process of life review again! I asked myself questions as everything I encountered became a "teacher" to me.

How will I live from the heart? I wrote. Then I answered my own question in the first of several philosophical messages from my heart:

> *I think it will happen to me as I continue to heal parts of me and live in my truth. I believe solitude is the key to balance. I must have enough time to pray, commune with nature, and listen. I am more and more willing to let go of the past and accept a new future. In some ways, this year of turning fifty years old is the most exciting and wonderful of my life. I am indeed forming my own design, my own rootedness, and I am choosing what I want in my life.*

> *I am experiencing the dignity that I find so imperative for human beings and the breath of life. With dignity, integrity and honesty can flow. Pull the dignity, and the dark side of a person — the shame, the survival, the anger and rage — will surface and become active participants. The dignity of a human being is a God-given right. The way of the heart is what Jesus came to teach us. It is the pathway to giving and receiving*

dignity. I want to continue to move my life more and more toward my home in my heart, where I will again feel the alignment of my existence with all of creation!

Early on a Saturday morning, I arose to see the sun rising. The music in my soul reached an emotional high that day. After getting a cup of coffee, I built a fire and listened to Pachelbel's "Canon in D," the song I played while doing journal writing.

As I look out the window across from me, I see the reflection of the fire. The leaves and trees look happy again. They have light and warmth. But the knowing is there. It is almost over. The fall, their time of exquisite beauty, is peaking and will be desolately gone soon. But for now, just let me put the pen down a moment and savor this.

I went outside and inhaled the beauty: the smell of a fall morning just screaming its crescendo, the golden aura that invited me to its radiant healing, the warm cup of coffee I held against my chest in the crisp, cool air. The contrast is what I love the most. It felt so fully healing, so full of life, so embracing. I didn't feel anger, sadness, wanting. I got tears just over the beauty of it. All of this, right here and now, is what I came for. I wanted to stop my life at that moment and just be "this" forever. What is heaven like? Is death like the crescendo of fall? I have now had the most paradise-like experience I have ever had in my life. How can I continue to find this in my life? By listening to the music of my soul; by hearing the beckoning call and responding to it and through the opening of my heart. I can find my soul where my creativity lies. Inviting that out is where paradise continues to exist in this life for me.

Fear encroached on me again, and I wondered what I would find when I opened into my creativity. I commented in my journal, "One always wonders—is there anything there? I think Persephone's gift through the mandala was to show me what *is* there. Maybe she left so I wouldn't just sit on that or be immobilized by that but rather have to go back into the well again."

More thoughts poured out on the pages of my journal:

While getting ready this morning, a thought came to me that seemed to fill me with Grace — "Renaissance." I am preparing as much as I can to jump into my own Renaissance. I need to look at my life with some scrutiny today as I decide or claim what I need to ask forgiveness for, and then I need to forgive myself. I want to move into an emptying meditation, a plea for Grace. Then I want to remember and recognize that which gives me joy and life. I want to write it, draw it, and honor it. Then I want to find a way to weave this learning into my "renaissance of becoming." It looks so exciting and so inviting that way. It is something to move toward, not away from. It is like "being with" the love of God instead of focusing on "moving away from" sin.

Yes, this moment requires commitment and discipline to keep it energized. But it requires love, community, nature, prayer, and most of all, Grace for it to flower and give its fragrance back to the world. In a sense, that is a beautiful way to make the soft road to death at the same time as becoming. So much like the leaves on the trees as they move into their full radiance in the fall — giving us so much energy, pleasure, and light — before they let go, die, and move into the darkness and cold and offer themselves to the Universe to feed the living through the nourishment they give. How much leaves are teaching me! They are teaching me the sacred role of the elegant crescendo and how this ritual of such great intensity is so "right" before they let go to move into the greater sharing of themselves.

Life and death, death and life –

the themes just kept repeating themselves for me with my inner messages finding any way possible to come out. The urgency of just a short time left pushed me to express myself. Finally, just nine days before leaving my home in the woods, I sat down in front of a black piece of paper to let the new mandala out. It took three sittings to finish. I was no longer hesitant to move further into my own healing. The experience of creation was very powerful. I felt the energy pushing it out of me. It was different from the first Persephone. The colors didn't seem as vibrant because the paper was a lower quality. However, "at night under the light," I wrote, "it becomes!" So I sat with it, absorbed it, and then let it speak to me.

The mandala incorporates several images that held symbolic messages for me. First, the heart in the center was key. The heart's colors appear in other places in the mandala. Red, the color for life, and green, the color for healing, fill the heartspace. The heart is surrounded by what was originally a ribbon, but later seemed like an umbilical cord. This ribbony form portrays great symbolic imagery: an angel, a person lying prone on the floor, a goddess, or a pitcher. Roots are growing from the heart's top and bottom through the form. A main root, at the bottom, looks older and less radiant than the others. A shape I call "The Bowl of Life" appears

at the bottom left of the figure, reflecting some of the same colors as the heart. Life flows from the ribbon along the left side into a sprig of berries, possibly pomegranate seeds or a sign of spring, of renaissance. Finally, deeply colored energy bursting into flames penetrate the boundary of the mandala circle on the right side.

The Bowl of Life is the soul. It is resting on the feminine side of the circle. The colors there are yellow, gold, pink, and white. It also reflects the masculine with the purples. What I call the "Hosts of Life" embraces the purple, red, and pink mixture of the masculine and feminine. The Bowl of Life is a beautiful integration of both masculine and feminine.

The round berries in the upper left sometimes remind me of Persephone and the importance of darkness and how it contributes to the whole. Or is this a sign of New Life, the Renaissance, emanating from the passion and healing flowing to it? It is the happiest part of the drawing.

The right side is active, flowing. It has a mind and beauty of its own, flowing right through the boundary of the drawing. The colors are so rich and alive. I pictured fire, and felt fire, when doing the mandala. The right side put the fire in me to complete the other side.

The greens at the top encompass safety. When I view this area, I sense the love in this drawing. It is like the Strength of God telling me in such a lovely strong color that I am safe and that I matter. A voice is telling me to just wait and listen, and my God will be there. The flames are all different colors of the rainbow. Their oranges and reds are very intense. They seem to hint of real pain. The flames flow into the roots at the top and bottom to give life and sustenance.

All of the roots have not yet grown through the cord, except at the top. I wondered what they would need to grow more. The big root is through—older and now, surrounded by younger, fresher supportive roots, beginning to grow.

A healing heart, the Bowl of Life, the integration of both masculine and feminine, symbols of darkness and new life, the new rootedness—all in a drawing filled with flow and intensity. This was the new picture of myself.

"It feels like I have turned myself inside out," I journaled. "My inner self is alive! The feminine needs more time and attention, and the masculine energy is there to fuel the process."

The mandala process took great faith and courage, and I was relieved and excited when it was finished. I needed more time to become more fully rooted, but the process was well underway.

Approaching the last week, my questions continued. Why is God so big to me? What is the fear inside me? I kept hearing the invitation to open to the Grace. The space between the bigness and my existence was beginning to connect.

My final reflection envisioned the second month in the woods as a microcosm of the second half of life:

> I am cherishing the ending of this holy time here in Door County. Even as it is ending, I seem to be loving each moment with a ravishing hunger, almost more intently than when it started. Is this like the process of dying? Has the last month been like the second half of life, where aliveness accentuates itself with the core beauty of life, found in the stillness and the connection with nature's gifts? I think so.

Receiving Grace

Fling wide the gates,

open the ancient doors,

and the Holy One will

come in.

—Psalm 24

Energy and inspiration seemed to guide my soul.

The last week of my journey was full in so many ways. Clearly I didn't know what was ahead of me, but I accepted that I would get the direction I needed if I continued to listen to that Inner Voice. I was settled about my plans to finish my degree. That seemed absolutely right. Beyond that, I knew that I needed to listen carefully and respond when I felt moved to do so.

As often happens, I was drawn to books that seemed absolutely perfect for what I needed. A book that attracted my attention was *Living Buddha, Living Christ*, by Thich Nhat Hanh. Some of the messages were so connecting at a time when affirmation of my experience was powerful. The author states:

When He [Jesus] opened His heart, the door of Heaven was opened to Him. . . . He was human, but, at the same time, he became an expression of the highest spirit of humanity. We are in touch with the highest spirit in ourselves, we too are a Buddha, filled with the Holy Spirit, and we become very tolerant, very open, very deep, and very understanding.[16]

He goes on to further state:

We do not have to die to arrive at the gates of Heaven. In fact, we have to be truly alive. The practice is to touch life deeply so that the Kingdom of God becomes a reality. This is not a matter of devotion. It is a matter of practice. The Kingdom of God is available here and now because God the Son is made of the energy of the Holy Spirit. He is the door that allows us to enter the Kingdom of God.[17]

I felt truly guided. Earlier I had found the book about woman being the image of the Holy Spirit. Now I was receiving a further understanding of the Holy Spirit, with a profound invitation, through the Spirit, to receive the Love of Christ.

Then another invitation presented itself. Energy was very active now! My friend Jean had reconnected with an old friend who now lived in Door County. She had become a Reiki Master and was offering a class on Level One Reiki. I had always been inspired by the vision of Jesus' healing touch. Also, living alone, I learned to appreciate touch as something essential for human beings to feel alive and loved. With that in mind, I accepted the invitation to join Jean in the training.

Although I felt some anxiety regarding the unknown as Jean and I approached the session, I had no idea what adventure was ahead for me. Three of us joined Ia, the Master, at her house for the all-day training session.

Ia explained the concept of the healing energy of Reiki. She took about three hours to talk with us and gently explain the process. From the very beginning I sensed a strange connection between Ia and me. I wondered if I had known her before. Also,

I felt the memory of my mother in the room. What does she have to do with Ia, I wondered?

During a break, Ia approached me and shared with me the connection she was feeling. Since we both accepted the possibility of past life experiences, we concluded that we had been related, most likely sisters. When I told her about my mother, she simply replied, "Perhaps your mother has something to say to you." With hope and curiosity, I accepted what she said.

After the break, we reached the point of what is called "Attunement." This is the receiving of the Reiki energy as a channel of healing. Ia stood behind me and did the ritual, which involved the movement of energy through breathing.

I felt my heartspace open, and I offered the most profound prayer of my life to receive healing. In the depth of that moment, I received Grace—the "confirmation" of my willingness and commitment.

The rest of the process was, for the most part, uneventful. Ia offered another Reiki session as part of the training package in which she would work with us on special issues in our lives, using some past-life regression if we were interested. Jean and I scheduled a full session for Monday.

I knew the session with Ia would be deep for me. I was anxious about it, but I trusted Ia, perhaps because of the personal connection I felt with her. Monday came, and with great anticipation Jean and I were back at Ia's home. When I walked in, Ia mentioned that she saw resistance, and I knew she meant from me. I could sense the resistance throughout my body. I was frightened.

When it was my turn, I proceeded to get up onto the massage table. I explained to Ia that I wanted to know more about my relationship to my original family. The Reiki meditation we did together was long, and one of the most profound experiences of my life. Apparently, I was willing, because after she guided me in the early part of the meditation, I spoke from that point on. I told her what I saw. Many elements came out as the story unfolded. What was important was that early on I experienced a birthing process. I found myself in a cave-tunnel. As I walked through that tunnel, light shone ahead of me so I always knew where I was going. Then suddenly, there was no light. I was terrified and completely alone. It touched me emotionally, and I cried, saying "I am always alone." Suddenly, there was a reflection on the wall of the cave-tunnel. It was a picture of Mary. The profile showed her kneeling and praying. She was there for me. Ia asked what I wanted to do. "Move on," I said. And I did.

Almost immediately I could see the light coming from the other side. I felt a pull. I literally felt my feet being pulled by some energy I couldn't see. I moved through the rest of the cave-tunnel very rapidly and was born. In the story, my mother had died while I was a baby, under less-than-amicable circumstances with my father. I was raised away from my father. Toward the end of the dream, I found my father again. We were united and happy to find each other. My mother came to me in spirit. She wanted to tell me something. She told me that she had forgiven my father. She was enjoying the fruits of heaven, and she had prepared a place for my father. She wanted me to tell him that she was waiting for him, and that he shouldn't worry about death. She would be there for him and take him on to New Life.

I was exhausted at the end of this meditation. I cried as hard as I ever have in my life. The fear of what was happening to me, along with the complete emptying of my pain and sadness, was incredibly difficult. I felt like I existed on several levels at one time. Coming back was a bit foreign and took some adjustment. However, I could see that some of my loose ends were now tied together. After so much time thinking about my mother as well as my father, this story was so healing for me. I needed to know that they were healed. That seemed necessary for my own healing process. And I no longer carried fear regarding my own death. Even though what I experienced was a birth, it didn't feel much different from a death experience. Most important, I met my inner guide, Mary, who will be there for me as she has been all along.

Ia was very gentle as we finished. She affirmed that I had done incredibly deep work, and that I needed to take care of myself. "Drink lots of water, eat, and rest," she advised. I did, but I found myself to be rather ungrounded and tired for about four days. She also suggested writing down the story so I would remember. She expected that the meaning of the story would unfold for some time. And it has!

Since that day, I have practiced Reiki almost every day. I find it to be such a warm and loving Energy. I am able to center fairly easily when I take the time to experience this Energy. It is a channel for remembering the gifts of my time in Door County where I believe I met the Spirit of God.

8

The Passage

Stand still. The trees ahead and the bushes beside you
Are not lost. Wherever you are is called Here,
And you must treat it as a powerful stranger,
Must ask permission to know it and be known.
The forest breathes. Listen. It answers,
I have made this place around you.
If you leave it, you may come back again, saying Here.
No two trees are the same to Raven.
No two branches are the same to Wren.
If what a tree or a bush does is lost on you,
You are surely lost. Stand still. The forest knows
Where you are. You must let it find you.

—David Wagoner
"Lost"
Traveling Light: Collected and New Poems [18]

Endings can often reveal the sweetest blessings.

It was almost time to leave. I had only two days left. I was ready for the final steps of the ritual.

Ritual had carried me through several transitions during the last year or more. For example, when I returned home from my recent divorce hearing, my friends welcomed me. They placed a white scarf on me to signify a life passage. We read poetry and prayed for all of us involved in this painful separation. We walked through the house to the rhythm of lovely, healing music and blessed rooms in the house as they filled with new life energy. It was this ritual that allowed a closing for me and a reconnection with hope through the loving support of my friends.

Leaving Door County also needed closure. I began to hug trees on my walks. I thanked the trees in my favorite places of quiet reflection. I took pictures of many places about which I had fond memories. This included a treehouse Jean and I discovered on one of our final walks around the lake, a symbol affirming the completion of this journey.

The last day prior to departure, I decided to deeply clean my little house in the woods to show my care and gratitude, and as a blessing for this sacred space. First, I built a fire in the fireplace and sat beside it. I talked to the Universe and promised to listen. I told the Universe how much I wanted to serve it and asked for the grace to hear what I needed to hear. I asked for the grace of courage to respond to what I heard. I thanked the house for the space it had given me to rest, reflect, and become. I reflected on how wounded I was as a result of losses over the last year. I recognized that there was now a softness around my healing heart. I gave thanks.

After this reflective time, I began to clean. I cleaned mindfully for the first time in my life, and actually enjoyed the process! It took most of the day and when it was finished, I was ready to let go.

On October 31st, I woke up early. It was the end, and yet I knew it was the beginning. The day started with breakfast with my friend Jean, who was also leaving that day to live with her sister for the winter. As we sat at our table looking out the window, we saw snowflakes gently dropping from the sky. That was our sign. The fall had ended!

I went back to the house for some last-minute tasks. I said one final prayer of blessing and left, leaving the locked door behind me. I headed to the real estate office to return the keys. I was ready for the final departure.

One more ritual seemed appropriate. I took pictures of other favorite places which I had not yet photographed, beginning with the real estate office, then the Red Oak Gift Shop where Jean had worked, then the wildly moving water in Ephraim. Those spots were followed by the post office, where I received loving letters and cards daily; the small deli, where I had bought cappuccino regularly; the dress shop I frequented all too often; and the grocery store that felt like community to me.

Egg Harbor was the last city to drive through before officially leaving the resort area of Door County. I expected tears, but that didn't happen. Instead, I was suddenly filled with euphoria — like something really good was going to happen to me. I felt the boon of Energy pushing me forward now that the trees had found me!

I thought of Persephone and her trip every time she returned from the Underworld. Nothing looked different, yet everything was changed. I was en route with the gifts I had been given to help navigate the rest of my life. With Persephone in my heart, I was going home!

PERSEPHONE –
Come Back from the Underworld

I am Persephone,
  come back from the underworld!
How do I live up here?
How do I bring to this world
  all that I have met below?

I am Persephone,
  come back from the underworld!
How do I be up here?
How do I create in this world
  the new reality
  from all that I have learned –
  cellularly learned –
  in the center of the Earth?

I am Persephone,
  come back from the underworld!
How do I navigate my way in this
world?
How do I honor and live by my
commitment
  in the face of whatever?
    My commitment,
    woven and rewoven moment by
      moment . . .
  to stay rooted in the truth
  at the deep center
  of my dark labyrinths within.

Those in the upper world
  allow their terror to paint
  my journey as a rape and abduction
  into the underworld,
  as though it were some evil place.
My descent, in truth,
  is voluntary –
  whether consciously so or not.

Those in the upper world
  who haven't been to the underworld
  and returned,
Pretend, no! they believe
  that the return is done with ease.
  That it is sweet simplicity,
  like, they imagine,
  the crocuses moving their way
  up through the newly thawed
  ground.

Those in the upper world
  assert that once returned,
  the journey is simply a dance in
  the blossoming garden.
They ask me to emerge instantly
  skipping, singing, happily,
  spreading cheer wherever I go.
They have no conception
  of the journey I've taken.
  They cannot imagine,
  out of their own fears,
  out of their own lack of experience,
  how many layers of defenses
  I have released in my descent.
They have no way to know
  how bare I have been stripped.
They don't want to know
  how raw I am as I return
undefended,
  or how painful the world up here
  feels to my sensitive, raw skin.

They ask me to return to the life
   I lived before.
What illusion! And what imposition!

Why would I want to go through the
deep,
   transformative journey into my own
   underground labyrinths,
   only to come back and act the same
   as I did before,
   only to come back to being who I
   was
   before my descent?
The journey is so deep,
   with such profound passages and
      pathways!
Having given myself so committedly
   in the underworld, in my own
   underground,
   I would experience the agony of self
   betrayal
   if I simply returned to my previous
   self –
As if that were even possible!

Had anyone told me where I was
going
   before I left for the underworld ...
   would I have gone?
Yes! Certainly yes!
   It was a call that had no "no."

Had anyone told me what I would
face
   on my return to this world ...
   would I have gone?
   Or more aptly,
   would I have come back?

Yes – hesitantly yes.
   Though it has taken
   trust in my Self and my guidance
   and such profound courage –
      courage being forged as each
         movement
         came and went!
It has taken profound allowing:
   I can no longer move my Self,
   but instead
   must allow my Self to move me.

Had anyone told me how many people
would
   be frightened of how I was living
   and the life I was calling them to ...
   would I have been able to bear it?
Had anyone told me I would need
   to walk again and again
   through the door to aloneness
   to live from my roots ...
      would I have been able to
      bear it?

Had anyone told me
   going through my own descent and
   return
would teach others – longing to learn –
and draw to me people who cherish
   all the truth and life that I most
   love ...
      would I have been able to bear it?

Had anyone told me who I would be
as my journey unfolded –
who I would grow,
who I would heal,
who I would shed,
who I would inhabit –
would I have believed it?
Yes and no!

Yes and no!
I already Knew
and yet could barely imagine
living as I am,
Living as I am
only because it is true for me
and so, must be done!

I am Persephone,
come back from the underworld.
How can I help in this world?
What will unfold and emerge next ...
as I honor and follow my
commitment
to live in this world
from the center of my being,
to create my world here
from the roots I have developed
there?

–Judith Barr[19]
Copyright © 1994,
revised 1996

Conclusion

BEFORE I LEFT FOR
MY FALL SABBATICAL, I MET WITH MY
newly appointed college advisor. I asked if
we could design a course for credit around
my upcoming experience in the woods. He
responded with interest, enthusiasm, and
support. We pondered on what to name
the course. Then his face changed to a
knowing look, and he said, "We will call it
'The Heroine's Journey'" (changed to "The
Healing Journey" in 2019). I could feel it
inside—what he suggested was right.

I didn't know how deep the journey
would be for me. I understand the depth of
it much more after reading my journals in
preparation for this book. It was a strange
experience to review my own thoughts
from the "morning pages." I felt like an
observer critiquing myself. It was itself a
ritual to help me put closure on that part of
my healing.

At times the task of telling this story
seemed overwhelming to me. Then I remem-

bered how I approached the mandala process, just one step at a time. It wasn't helpful to start with the end in mind. I was more comfortable just starting, being in the moment with each chapter as it unfolded. This is one of the greatest lessons I have learned:

Trust the process.
Enjoy the moment. Be!

Recurring themes surfaced as I read through my journal and reflections. I appreciate the choice I now have to live my life as who I am, remembering how precious that is, and honoring it in the way I live. However, the most important gift is the connection to my soul that I found in the silence. Continuing to find quiet time is a priority. No longer can I choose to give it all away!

On March 22, 1997, I will be fifty years old. It is time to move on and begin the adventure of the second half of my life!

Part Two

JOURNEYS
OF
REBIRTH

Introduction

DUANE TRAMMELL

GINNY'S TWO MONTHS IN THE WISCONSIN WOODS PROVIDED A TIME for her to pause and reflect on the unexpected changes that occurred in her life, listen more attentively to what her soul was telling her, and plan the next steps for her new life.

My business colleague Mike Blevins teaches leadership skills in workshops. After he teaches a series of competencies, he asks a question that I have also adopted: "So what? Why is this important for me to know?" You may be thinking, "Ginny's story is interesting, but her situation isn't like mine. Where's the part in this book that tells me what I should do?"

Part Two of *Wisdom from the Woods* will help you answer that question. In chapter 9, we share the stories of three colleagues after they read "The Healing Journey." Each story has a tragic or unfortunate event that triggered a need for retreat, reflection, and finding a way to survive the incident. Not all transitions arise from negative events, but many do. When these troubling times come, most of us want to run away from them as quickly as possible. If we have the courage to pause, reflect, and listen to what our soul is telling us, we can learn from these events and emerge stronger.

When I first read "The Healing Journey" in 2016, I was searching for ways to grow in wisdom and emotionally ready myself for the heartbreaking, terminal illness of my friend and business partner, Ann McGee-Cooper. Ginny's time in the woods provided a model for me. In chapter 10, we share how you can create your own process to face your personal challenges. Choose the elements of retreat that work for you and order them in the sequence that is most meaningful. It works differently for each of us; we invite you to build your personal plan.

Chapter 11 tells the story of what happened in the twenty-three years after Ginny's discovery of wisdom in the little cabin in the woods. What she created was inspiring, remarkable, and has helped hundreds of people. The insights gained from this chapter will help you see that we will face many changes in our lifetime, not just one transition. Ginny tells us:

> There have been so many times when things don't happen the way we would want them to and we are disappointed. We are forced into a transition we hadn't planned. Years go by, and one day we look back and realize that good things came from that difficult period of our lives and that maybe what did emerge was actually better than our own initial plan. Sometimes we grow into a new way of serving others or we begin to heal and eventually find that we can embrace a new relationship. There are times we wait, pray, read, and reflect . . . and lo and behold

. . . *the retirement we were so afraid of starts to find form in a way that gives us joy like we had never had before! There have been several times in my life when I felt the world had ended. And with time, in some way or another, I found ways to reconnect with that Inner Light within and my spirit started to find new life and hope.*

Integrating the practices of "The Healing Journey" into your own life will help you find the quiet spaces that are necessary to

move major life changes out of your head into your heart, for in the heart is where wisdom is born.[20]

Embracing Transformation

Thoughts from OUR CONTRIBUTORS

AS GINNY AND I HAVE PUT THE expanded version of this book together, we have shared copies of the original "The Healing Journey" (HJ), engaged in wonderful conversations, and interviewed others who have gone through major transitions in their lives. We chose to include three of those stories to encourage you in your own journeys of transformation.

The first story comes from Steve Thiry, recently retired assistant chief of police in Fond du Lac, Wisconsin. In his retirement, Steve is assuming a new role with Sophia Transformative Leadership Partners, serving as the program director and a learning facilitator. Previously, Steve served on the Sophia board of directors for nearly seven years. In this HJ transition story, Steve tells a powerful account of a tragic event that changed his life.

The second story is written by Matthew Kosec—a business colleague, friend, and an invested learning partner for both Ginny and me. Matt is "the real deal." He is a sought-after organizational development consultant and inspiring speaker. What makes him the real deal is his authentic vulnerability. In his HJ transition story, Matt opens his heart to us during a challenging time in his life.

Our final story is from Deborah Welch. Deborah is an award-winning faculty member at Capella University, teaching "The Psychology of Leadership" and guiding dissertation research in the area of self-awareness and leadership. Ginny and Deborah have been friends and learning partners for over twenty years, supporting one another's dreams in yearly retreats. These retreats allow for time to listen to their hearts and share what is calling to them. Deborah is currently intrigued by dream work and shows how it can be helpful and healing in navigating life's unexpected challenges.

STEVE THIRY

Called to Serve

I had always viewed the month of March as a time without much significance.

As a non-Irishman, even St. Patrick's Day came and went without too much celebration. For some years, March signaled the end to the winter season, bringing hope of spring and a season of new growth. Other times, March was an extension of a long winter, delaying the return of new life. Either way, March only had significance as it related to the seasons and the transition from one season to another.

On March 20, 2011, at about 6:30 a.m., the significance of March changed for me. I remember being at my in-law's cottage and being awakened by my sister-in-law. I could tell by her serious voice that something was wrong and work was trying desperately to reach me. When I answered the phone, I recognized the familiar voice of the captain of detectives. His voice was somber, and he simply stated, "Steve, we have shots fired and two officers are down. It's not good." With this news, my heart sank and it felt like I was swallowing a rock. I told the captain I was at the cottage, but I was on my way. As I hung up the phone, the only thought on my mind was "how fast can I get there from here?"

I remember driving down the interstate at a rate much too fast for the speed limit, watching for other police officers and hoping they would not be paying too much attention to traffic on a Sunday morning. I called ahead to see if I could get more information from anyone at the police department. The only person I could reach was another captain who was on scene. I spoke with him for a few moments before he said he had to go because the ambulance he was in was taking fire. I told him to hang up and get to safety. I felt powerless and ashamed that I was not there helping my fellow officers in this great time of need. Several questions hounded me: "How can I get there faster?" "Why was I at the cottage during this time of need?" "You are supposed to have your partner's back . . . where are you when they need you?"

When I arrived at the scene, things were chaotic. I tried my best to find an assignment, but no one had prepared us for this. Never in my wildest dreams did I think I would ever be thrown into an incident hours after it had started, with little to no communication to establish incident command.

Things did not change after receiving word that the danger at the scene was over. The aftermath included the death of Officer Craig Birkholz and life-threatening injuries to Officer Ryan Williams and to our K-9 Grendal. The hours following the "all clear" entailed my assisting the Department of Criminal Investigation with their investigation of the shooting, Critical Incident Stress Debriefings with those on scene, and establishing a plan to screen officers to see if they were ready to return to duty. The first sixteen hours of the day were a whirlwind. All I really remember is toward the end of the day, when most of the others had gone, I sat alone in the Emergency Operations Center watching the news coverage from the shooting and breaking down in tears. After I pulled myself together, I drove home. It was late, but my wife and daughter were waiting up for me. My wife said our daughter would not go to sleep until she had seen her dad and knew he was okay. Hearing this, I broke down in tears again. I had no idea how such an event could affect everyone, including our children.

Relentless Pain

The following days brought about a lot of one-on-one interviews with officers who were on scene the day of the shooting. Everyone wanted and needed to talk about what they had gone through. Many cried while recounting what they had seen and the horror they had experienced. I could not help but cry myself as I listened to my friends relaying words carrying such pain. I could feel the pain even though I was not there during the actual event. I remembered the pain of a close loss I felt many years earlier with the unexpected death of my best friend and then my own sister a few years later. I knew the hurt these officers were feeling, and hearing it in their voices brought that pain back again for me.

It took a long time for our department to heal from this tragic day. Almost everyone had to dig deep to determine whether or not performing this job was worth it. Many with children wondered what would happen to their kids if they died at work. Who would take care of their loved ones? We lost some officers because of this event. Some, near retirement, jumped at the chance and left the profession. Others, who weren't eligible for retirement, simply resigned and found other jobs. Still others lost their way and ended up leaving the profession via other means. Nonetheless, the majority of officers in the department, despite what they had seen, remained. The call to serve and protect was just too strong for them to walk away. What amazing people. These are the people I needed to serve as best I could. They deserved nothing less.

A few years went by and while no one would ever forget what happened on March 20th, the department seemed to be back on its feet and moving forward. We learned some things that tragic day and began training harder to ensure we would be prepared should such an event take place again. I think some officers believed March 20th was a once-in-a-career event and took comfort in the fact that there was no way it would be repeated in their lifetime.

On the afternoon of March 24, 2015, I had driven home to change clothes and pick up my wife. We were planning on returning to Fond du Lac to attend a public safety appreciation dinner at the Knights of Columbus Hall. It had always been a nice event and a social time to interact with all of the other police and fire agencies throughout the county. We were on the interstate near north Fond du Lac when I received a phone call from our SWAT commander. He asked me what was going on in the city. I had not heard anything, but he had gotten word that something big was happening, and he thought the SWAT team might be called out. Then we both received the SWAT page and ended our call so he could respond. The message said something like "shooting incident in the area of Pick and Save on North Berger Parkway." We were only minutes from that location. I told my wife we would not be attending the dinner. I was in civilian clothes and not armed, so we had to drive past the scene to get to the police department. I had my wife drop me off and told her to take a safe route back home. I can't image what was going through her mind during that drive back.

By the time I put together a weapon, vest, and badge the only thing I could do on scene was deliver the command post. I dropped it off, and then I was told Trooper Trevor Casper had been killed during a shootout with a suspect. Once again, there was nothing I could do.

I was asked to return to the police station and be the liaison with the Wisconsin Law Enforcement Death Response Team. This meant I needed to find a room and get coffee for the team members. That was the extent of my involvement in this call. This did not sit well with me. Yet another tragedy when I wanted to be there for my team, but all I could do to help was get coffee. Apparently, I was not the only one with this concern. When the shooting occurred, several Fond du Lac officers were within a block of where Trooper Casper died but could do nothing to stop it. I can't even speak to what the troopers who were actually with

Trevor must have been going through. This was March 20, 2011, all over again. Once again, I cried with my fellow officers over the death of one of our brothers.

Deep Questions

Starting back in 2013, the department began dealing with numerous internal matters regarding personnel issues. Establishing shared core values and accountability was paramount to culture change within the department. One of these personnel issues came to a head, and there was a turn of events. The issue went to litigation, questioning the morals and ethics of management and the very core values that drive us. To top it off, the union made a public statement against management and in favor of the employee who had brought dishonor to our core values. All of this was almost unbearable to me. I had the undesirable responsibility of conducting internal investigations for eight years. It was my job to police the police, holding our officers accountable to themselves, each other, and the community we serve. It was a difficult task heaped with negativity and questioned motives. Despite this, I performed this duty to the best of my ability knowing that this was a way for me to serve the community. They deserved no less. In addition to internal matters, I was also tasked with taking care of the officers most in need following both of these shootings. These people were my friends — my brothers and sisters. Now, some of these very same people turned and questioned my motives. Even more troubling was that they questioned my own integrity and ethics. This all but broke me.

I spent many nights lying awake trying to make peace with what was happening. I could see how these matters were affecting my life at home and my relationship with my wife and daughter. I shared with my wife how heavy my heart was and that I wondered if I could stay in the department I had grown to call my family. My sense of self-esteem and belonging were gone. My purpose was to serve those officers under my command, and yet if they were questioning my intentions, how could I stay? If I left, how would I support my family? I was not at retirement age yet, and leaving would directly impact our financial well-being.

This was my state of mind, when the five-year anniversary of Officer Craig Birkholz's death arrived. The department planned to attend a church service on the actual date of his death. The weeks leading up to the anniversary caused me to revisit questions I had been wrestling with since 2011. How long do we do this? Who do we serve by holding these memorials? Is it for us to feel better, or is it for the family to somehow heal and move forward? Does this help, or does it just reopen the wound all over again, leaving an enormous scar and emotional damage? Can I even think about not attending as a leader in this department? Will my absence be seen as uncaring to those who need these events? What about me? How can I best heal and go forward?

Against what my heart was telling me, I decided to go to the memorial service. As a department leader, I was supposed to be there despite what I thought I needed. My wife and daughter didn't even hesitate when I asked them to attend. Without discussion they both said "sure."

When we arrived at the church that Sunday morning, there didn't seem to be many people there. My first instinct was to say, "See, I'm not the only one who wants to move on." As we waited in the gathering area, more and more people from the department arrived with their families. Soon, quite a crowd had gathered.

Everyone there commented on how brilliant the morning sun was that day. As you looked to the east, the sunshine pouring in through the windows was blinding. Comments were made about how spring was finally here.

It was time for the service to start, so we all entered the church and took our reserved seats to the left of the altar. I was in the second row behind the chief's family and the city manager. The intense sunlight was shining brilliantly on the first and second rows and directly on me and my family. I remember feeling how warm the light was on my face and wondering how I would make it through the service without melting. I needed to avert my eyes as the light was just too bright.

The homily of the Catholic Mass is where I do much of my reflecting. On this day, the homily was replaced by the reading of the Passion since it was Palm Sunday. As the priest and members of the congregation read their respective parts, I thought about the Passion, my conflicted view of the department, and what I was going to do. While pondering these things, I heard the words of Christ as he prepared for his task the night of Holy Thursday. I heard his prayers to God asking for help but yielding to his will. I heard Christ's words to his apostles. Then I heard of the betrayal, the suffering, and death of Christ. During this Mass, I also thought of Craig and the suffering and sacrifice he had made five years earlier. Then it sank in. Jesus was telling me that all he was trying to do was serve mankind when he walked the earth as a man. What he received in return was ridicule, suffering, and a painful death. Even so, he never stopped serving and yielded to God's plan and will. Craig was also telling me something. He was telling me that he had tried to serve the people of Fond du Lac as best he could. What he received in return was to be killed tragically in the prime of his life, leaving behind a wife, parents, and a brother. When I compared these sacrifices to what I was experiencing, I heard Jesus say, "Suck it up and get back in the fight," as if he were a tactical trainer trying to help me survive.

The Revelation

What I learned that day was that my suffering during all of this was nothing compared to the suffering others have endured while doing nothing more than trying to make a difference for others. If I am truly a servant-leader, I need to think of myself less, work harder, and honor those who have really sacrificed. To make a difference, you cannot quit when things get tough. Rather, you only make a difference if you push harder when things are tough. Otherwise, evil wins and it brings everyone down.

Coppell Police Chief Danny Barton welcomes Steve Thiry to the March 2019 Dallas SLLC® session

Reflecting back on my experience in church, I now believe that the sunlight that morning had significance. It was a sign of spring—a sign of hope, growth, and life. It also signified not just a changing of the season, but a change in my life, the life of the department, and the life of the world through the miracle of Easter. That brilliant light was a reminder that I am not alone. These thoughts came to me as I openly discussed my experiences with trusted friends who knew exactly what to ask to get me out of my own way and to move forward.

MATTHEW KOSEC

What the Soul Needs

Sometimes life has a strange way of just handing it to you.

After reading Ginny's winding, purposeful, path through "The Healing Journey," I was compelled to move beyond the role of a spectator. Etched in my mind is an image of me alongside her in Door County. I imagine us there, and she's sharing a passage from her writing with me: "Life can change in a moment!"

My moment, the moment that my life changed with brutal swiftness, is unmistakably connected to Duane's description of feeling "like the earth is swallowing us." During my moment I felt swallowed, digested, and . . . well, you know what comes next . . . by the world around me.

Like Ginny's invitation in "The Healing Journey," I also invite you to sit with me, just for a while, to peer into my inner journey. Although the moment that changed my life happened in 2013, the buildup started long before.

"I want it" + "I work for it" = "I get it"

My admiration of law enforcement officers began early in life, and during high school I wanted to get as close as I could to experiencing the life of a cop. In the rural area where I grew up, there were no formal programs to become engaged with law enforcement. That didn't stop me, and while I accessed all the officer "ride-along" programs I could, I craved more. With the urging and support of my parents, I asked to meet with Mel Mefford, then-Jefferson County, Washington, sheriff. Thanks to the sheriff's servant heart, I proudly strolled from his office with a custom-crafted high school internship program.

Next stop, college in Austin, Texas. With unwavering commitment to a path of police work, I obtained a Bachelor of Arts in Criminal Justice in under four years. An internship was required, but none of the available options attracted me, so I created my own. Fascinated by the Austin bar scene (and perhaps even partaking in said scene), I was interested in the Texas Alcoholic Beverage Commission (TABC). After a few cold calls, I met with then-TABC Lieutenant David Ferrero—yet another law enforcement leader who acted with a servant's heart. Once again, I emerged from an office with a newly minted internship.

If one were to follow this trajectory, it seems clear that entry into local law enforcement would come promptly after college graduation. It didn't. The young man who created two law enforcement internships from scratch, graduated in under four years with near-perfect grades, and whose public persona was everything law enforcement couldn't bring himself to apply to police departments.

Instead, I sold golf clubs.

For about nine months, I sold golf clubs. I didn't decide to do this to create the evident and often vocal bafflement of people close to me. Despite a few half-hearted attempts, I just couldn't bring myself to apply to a police department. It was inexplicable to my head and heart (at least then), but the drive wasn't there.

With time, though, my mind lost the ability to reconcile the career path interruption. I flipped a switch and aggressively applied to Dallas-area police departments. I was quickly hired by the Carrollton Police Department and entered the police academy.

The upward-focused and quick-paced career path resumed. I remember on the first day that I was allowed to drive the squad car, my field training officer asked me, "Do you have a career goal at Carrollton?" I calmly said, "I'd like to be chief." That comment was met with raucous laughter, followed by, "Let's just worry about not crashing this car."

After meeting the minimum service requirement of two years, I eagerly studied for the promotional test, prepared for the interview, and was rewarded with a remarkably quick promotion to sergeant. That same training officer attended my promotional ceremony. As he shook my hand in congratulation, he said,

"I remember you said you were going to be chief. My God, you weren't kidding."

No, I was not. Despite some officers I was supervising telling me, "Son, I have underwear older than you," I continued the rapid path to the top by being promoted to lieutenant a few years later.

None of this "path to the top" came easy; it was undergirded by taking on extra projects, an unwavering work ethic, and constant attention to goals. Yet a dangerous equation was forming in my head:

I want it + I work for it = I get it

Dangerous, because the underlying mathematical assumption was the "I" . . . the "I" that is in control of each part of the equation. In control of, well, everything.

Thanks to the mentorship of then-Assistant Chief Mac Tristan and the hard work of many officers at the Carrollton Police Department, we put the notion of front-line empowerment to work and achieved remarkable crime-reduction results. Our initiatives gained wide recognition, and I found myself on teams of presenters speaking at international conferences. I was proud of our accomplishments, all the time receiving further endorsement of my personal calculus: I want it + I work for it = I get it.

Mac moved on to become the police chief of nearby Coppell, Texas, creating a vacancy for my expected next promotion to assistant chief. Because I assumed my success formula was solid, it didn't matter that Carrollton also had a new police chief at that time. Certainly, he'd recognize talent and play his role in my well-defined path to the top.

He didn't, and I wasn't promoted.

Dig In, Fall Down

When faced with new data (no promotion) that does not fit our assumptions (my personal success equation), we only have two choices:

1. Reconsider the assumptions (my equation), or

2. Name the source of the new data as flawed or incorrect.

At the time, I saw nothing but ample evidence to support the second option. Obviously, this new chief didn't know talent when he saw it. (An important note: At the time of this writing, six years later and during a period of when many chiefs have come and gone, not only is he still there, but he's been promoted!)

"It isn't me; it's him." Before long, it became, "It isn't me; it's them."

When goals stem from a place of ego, proving long-held beliefs and assumptions becomes an intense mission. A mission that becomes, perhaps, even more important than the goals or assumptions themselves. I dug in and aggressively pursued this mission.

Undaunted, I applied for several executive-level police department positions around the country, willing to relocate my growing family. But we didn't need to move; soon I became deputy chief of police in Coppell, Texas, again working for Mac Tristan. I rested in the assurance that my career path had only experienced a momentary delay, and I had never really lost control of my bright future.

Then that bright future changed, as Ginny writes, "in a moment." Actually, through a series of moments in 2013, each one more effective than the last at replacing my pride, dignity, and dreams with pain and darkness.

A moment in which I made a critical mistake.

A moment in which I sat down with the director of Human Resources and signed a "Mutual Agreement of Separation."

A moment when the investigation became public, a news crew camera was on my doorstep, and the headline ran nationwide.

A moment when I knew I'd never be a police chief.

What the Soul Needs

My wife, Shannon, has often told me, "One way or another, whether you choose it or not, your soul will get what it needs."

"What the soul needs" is a silly notion for someone who works hard and is consistently rewarded with promotions. My personal equation did not require a soul. If I'm fully in control, why concern myself with such an abstract notion?

Well, that only works if one can maintain the illusion of full control. During 2013, my illusion of control was unmistakably shattered. National level attention for accomplishments had been replaced with national level attention of reported disgrace.

Shannon was right; my soul was claiming what was needed. I'd like to believe I would have accepted a subtler hint from my soul instead of this incredibly painful and public path. Except, when I add what happened in my life beyond pursuing becoming a police executive, an entirely different narrative emerges. My soul was loud and clear the whole time. I just wasn't listening.

Listening to the Soul

The difference now is that I'm learning to listen.

It started with a phone call from a dear mentor, Dr. Ann McGee-Cooper. We spoke on one of the most painful days, just as the separation from Coppell was unfolding. I contacted her for comfort, but it came in unexpected form. She reminded me that I wasn't that special: "Matt, unwieldy situations happen to good people all the time." She challenged me to write down my goals and dreams, even though at this time I was convinced they were dying. She told me to journal, writing questions with one hand and answering them with the other. Most powerfully, she decried my thinking that this pointed to my failure as a father: "This moment is the greatest opportunity you might ever have to teach your children how to live . . . and thrive . . . during the hardest times. Remember, it's okay for them to see you cry."

In the days following my formal separation from law enforcement I had an experience that seemed strange and abnormal. I felt a surge of energy, optimism, and enthusiasm. I told no one because on its face it didn't align with the painful and public separation.

I was hearing my soul.

Matthew, you are now free to pursue what is really in your heart, the real dreams and passions that truly light you up, not a formal position of power that is an illusion of success. You are free to pursue your truest passions and dreams!

Triggered by the necessity of resume preparation/writing, I began to reflect on my entire journey. Somewhere around 2000, I had met Ann and Duane, both of whom introduced me to the true power and depth of servant leadership, and they each grew to be my closest mentors. For more than a decade they invited me to present at seminars and write creative servant leadership content, and I seized every opportunity.

My personal interests were all about organizational life and leadership, only some of which were focused specifically on law enforcement. While many of my police peers grumbled about leadership books showing up on promotional exams, I was secretly thrilled.

> *Matthew, notice how much you love learning about leadership and the human experience? You are so excited when you get to write or teach with Ann or Duane. Do you notice that you spend your days off with them and see police work as an interruption?*

As a police lieutenant I was driven to learn more, and so I pursued a master's degree. While most of my peers did the same, they were studying topics like "emergency management" or "criminology." Without hesitation, I enrolled and graduated with a Master of Arts in organizational leadership, with an emphasis on servant leadership.

> *Matthew, when people ask you why you are working toward a leadership degree, do you notice how excited you are to tell them that leadership fascinates you and how you love helping others achieve their dreams regardless of the work they're doing?*

Unhealthy shame that lingers in our hearts can prevent us from receiving signals from our soul. It can be difficult to admit that what we've presented on our "outside" doesn't match what's "inside." It was incredibly hard to reflect back on my youth.

> *Matthew, do you notice that you started two internships from scratch? Did they really have anything to do with law*

enforcement, or was it more about creating something new
... being an entrepreneur?

Like Ginny's inner work discoveries, these reflections didn't happen all at once. They took time, and many came from reflections from people around me. Although I couldn't name it then, the energy and optimism I felt after leaving Coppell resulted from the freedom to do something new. This was a new sensation, allowed to emerge when I let go of the illusion of my personal "success equation." My choice was to either ignore this new awareness (again) or lean into it.

From the darkness and pain emerged opportunity. After nine grueling months of questioning if I was on the right path, I became a trainer for a national retail company. Opportunities to create and execute leadership conferences for hundreds of front-line leaders materialized. Work didn't feel like work, and I experienced the energy to accomplish things I never imagined. Although I had very little formal power or public recognition, I felt a filling of my soul that could only be possible with the concurrent emptying of my thirst for control.

Matthew, notice how you lose track of time, work endlessly,
and go home each day with a fuller heart when you are
serving others by helping them become better leaders,
thriving in their own journeys?

I discovered that when I am limited to my own controlling vision of the future, many opportunities remain hidden. With a bit of surrender, they become visible. In 2015 I was approached to lead a Dallas-icon restaurant and catering company that had practiced servant leadership for decades. I accepted, and relished the opportunity to learn every intricate detail of operating a multimillion-dollar business.

A New Equation

Through journaling and pursuing intentionally vulnerable relationships with generous and wise mentors like Ginny, Duane, and Deborah Welch, I started to, as Duane states, "Create [my] own way of listening to [my] inner teacher."

Most striking in Ginny's healing journey is that connecting with ourselves, doing the "inner work," and being open to "hearing" what is in our soul does not necessarily create inner peace. Quite the contrary. It can open the most frightening doors through which we never want to peer, let alone pass through.

Robert K. Greenleaf knew this when he wrote: "Awareness is not a giver of solace — it is just the opposite. It is a disturber and an awakener. Able leaders are usually sharply awake and reasonably disturbed. They are not seekers after solace. They have their own inner serenity."[21]

Resisting our awareness imprisons us in the illusion of control. It is our soul — our inner teacher — inviting us to surrender into the mystery of what's next. Thankfully, our soul is relentlessly persistent. As my wife's quote reminds me, it may drag us into what is needed. Our soul may even kick us square in the gut to be finally noticed. My soul seeks far more than mere success. The pursuit is toward, as Greenleaf described, my "own inner serenity."

Surrender is accepting that I'm not in control, but that doesn't absolve me of responsibility. I must do my part, including the hard work, new projects, and achieving personal goals. But my part is combined with what Ginny described as "ribbons of experiences [that] unfold and offer guideposts and lamplights to the rest of one's life."

A new equation emerges:

Hard Work (my part) + Surrender (inner teacher or soul) = Inner Serenity

After more than two years of leading a restaurant and catering company, many powerful "ribbons of experience" were evident. As hard as it was to accept, I admitted these ribbons weren't affirming my work.

Matthew, notice how you've returned to a stable, operations-focused place. One that is premised on moving upward in an organization. Is this releasing that passion and excitement that you've connected with all along?

Matt Kosec sharing servant leadership insights with a Dallas client

My inner teacher was speaking, and I was learning to trust. I had to make a change, especially since I know the depth of pain, loss, and grief of being dragged into necessary change by one's soul. It takes extraordinary strength to accept that all my needs and wants will flow from the pursuit of inner serenity. I'm certain my bank will not accept "inner serenity" as a form of mortgage payment. But surrender to our soul doesn't come with the luxury of control and certainty. Ginny learned to surrender to the movement of her hand in creating a mandala and Duane to a future without a dear mentor and business partner. Both acts of surrender led (are leading!) to incredible futures.

I resigned my position and launched my own servant leadership–focused consulting firm. It was time to honor that spirit of entrepreneurship and passion to help others along their journey of leadership and life. I'm so thankful to have stories like "The Healing Journey" to affirm and encourage my own journey.

DEBORAH WELCH

Awakening Through Dreams

If you can learn to live into your dream messages, a natural healing process happens.

In times of huge loss in my life, surprisingly, it has been journaling about my nighttime dreams that helped me find my way through the pain and confusion. Around 1985, I found a book that gave me guidance on how to journal about my dreams. I wrote out whatever came to mind when I woke up in the morning. I didn't write daily—sometimes once a week or once a month.

What I wrote down looked like chicken scratch. And, many times, the script of the dream made no sense. Sometimes I would have a nightmare I couldn't shake, so I would reluctantly record it, using the journaling process. Little did I know that I would find such grace through dreams, and that I would grow closer to my soul.

My Journey with Dreams

My time of loss happened in 1987, but I remember it like it was yesterday. My fiancé Bruce and I had a fight, and later I got a call at 3 a.m. that my car was totaled. The police officer told me Bruce was "in the morgue." I went into a state of shock. When the sun rose that morning, I couldn't believe it. How could life continue as if nothing had happened? People outside were getting into their cars and leaving for work and continuing with the motions of life. It all felt alien. I wanted to get off the planet. Grief poured through me and I felt empty, nauseous, fragile, and weak. How could I understand this tragedy in my life? The roots of my faith were shaken apart. A few weeks after the accident, I chose to stop my private practice as a psychotherapist. Even though clients were still having wonderful healing moments in our sessions, I felt I had nothing to give. I felt completely empty. I didn't know what was happening.

People around me tried to help in different ways. Some tried to distract me and encouraged me not to think about what had happened. Several friends told me not to blame myself, and one implied I was in a victim role and needed to stop. I tried going to a therapist and talking through my pain, but nothing was pulling me out of the numbness and self-deprecation I felt. Yet, during this time, I did keep up journaling my dreams. I wrote out all my feelings of immense sadness, anger, whatever. I asked myself questions like:

- What role was I playing in the dream?

- How was I feeling in the dream?

- How was the dream like waking?

- What can I learn from this dream from a perspective of deeper wisdom?

In other words, what would a wisdom figure tell me about this dream?

I wasn't trying to analyze my dreams. Instead, I was letting the metaphors and feelings speak to me. I learned to allow my feelings to unfold and run their full course in a dialogue between my Dreammaker and myself. Going on a journey with dreams can happen through art, meditation, dialoguing with others, hearing others' thoughts (like "if it were my dream . . ."), or asking questions through journaling.

Here is a snapshot of a dream inquiry from my journal:

Me: *My sadness feels immense. Will there ever be an end to the tears and pain? If only Bruce would come to me in a dream.*

Dream: *I have an experience of Bruce in my dream.*

Me: *Even though I had that great dream a week ago and I started feeling happier, now I am so sad again. Why did Bruce die and leave me?*

Dream: *Within the next series of dreams there is one where Bruce is with me in the dream. . . . He is a little bright sparkly light and he is so happy. I express I am angry with him; without*

his body here it is hard. I scream really loud. The anger I didn't
want to feel is all coming out.

Me: *Dreammaker, I am doing a lot of journaling on self-*
forgiveness. There is so much I wish I would have done
differently.

Dream: *I am with Bruce again. We are back in time, before his*
death. I know that he is going to die. I begin to think of how I
can respond differently so he will live. When I find him drunk,
I remain very calm and respond with love. He stands up to head
for the door. Instead of responding with further blame and
anger, I lovingly tell him I care: "Please stay." As the dream
progresses, I take every action that I can think of to do things
differently, to do things right, to be perfect . . . to account for
any error I thought I had made. Then suddenly I realize that in
spite of my much more loving response—even if I respond like a
saint—there is nothing I can do to stop this event. Bruce is
going to die. It is not in my power to change it and my actions
are inconsequential. Suddenly a weight lifts from my shoulders,
almost like being surrounded in light. I can feel all the guilt
inside release. I say to Bruce, "If you knew you were going to die,
what would you want me to know?" He replies, "I'd want you to
think of the image of who I am becoming." I feel a sense of joy
that perhaps his soul is living on in some new way.

The peace remained with me as I awoke. It was as if Bruce had
reached out and hugged and comforted me. The weight that lifted
off my shoulders—the new life and new joy that I found—amazed
me. I realized this wasn't about me at all. This was Bruce's life
path; it was between him and his soul. I was absolutely released
from the prison I had made. I hadn't realized I had such guilt until
it fell off my shoulders. A year later I met my husband, Thom.
My work catapulted into some of the most meaningful work in
my life, and it continues to evolve in the field of leadership.

Ginny's healing journey brought her ever closer to wisdom, love, and healing, as she journaled the question: "How will I live from the heart?" Similarly, this Dreammaker work has been an avenue for me to grow in my capacity to choose love over fear, and find my way to creative new beginnings.

Of course, I'm not the only one helped by dream work. It is widely known that dreams help balance your life and enable you to become more whole. A nightmare can awaken you out of a pattern that had been hurting you, and dreams can give you breakthrough answers to the most complex challenges. I know this from research and even more from my own personal journey and my work coaching others. I have seen the amazing answers that reside in people.

Dreams Can Open New Avenues

Stories from inspiring servant-leaders like Ann McGee-Cooper, Robert Greenleaf, and Gandhi affirm this. Ann observed that dreams are a quick way to find help as a servant-leader if you are overwhelmed. Her mentor, Robert Greenleaf, said dream work enlarged his awareness of his inner life and quickened his creativity.

Gandhi, facing a time of trauma in his country when there was torching, theft, and riots, had a dream that brought healing to India. He had tried speaking at public meetings, begging for change, attempting to get his letters published in newspapers. He felt helpless to solve the challenge. When he retreated to fast and pray, one night he dreamed that all of the warring religious factions in India had forsaken their own holy festivals in order to gather together in prayer and public procession on a single day.[22]

Inspired by his dream, Gandhi brought together nearly every religious leader in the country. Not only was violence reduced, but the various Indian factions opposing colonialism found a common voice – leading to nonviolent social change.[23]

Powerful dreams emerge when we are paying attention. And sometimes, like in Gandhi's dream, a breakthrough dream can awaken us to something that changes everything. My Bruce dream was like that. Its impact took me out of my self-imposed prison. I had forgotten how my feelings had unfolded in a series of dreams until I looked back at my journal, but the breakthrough dream image stayed with me year after year. A lesson from dream work: If you pay attention to your dreams you will get stronger messages and greater dreams. A natural healing process happens if you embrace your dream messages. Feelings will open up until you reach a place that is deeply peaceful and beautiful.

My Bruce dream is etched in my memory and continues to serve me. After my mother had a massive stroke, I experienced nine intense months as a caregiver. It was a time of great learning, a time when I never took one day for granted, and also one of the hardest times of my life. I noticed I was telling myself, "Can't you do more? What if you aren't doing enough?" The memory of my Bruce dream would pop into my mind and remind me that whatever I did, this was between my mom and her soul. What mattered was the love between us.

In easier times, dreams help me with creative ideas or warn me to steer clear of emotional and relationship patterns I don't need to repeat. In hard times of transition, dreams remind me not to deny the presence of a power much greater than myself. Learning to trust the wisdom I have inside when fears or trauma (or even small things) arise is still a process. I expect it to always be a mystery which involves inner work and growth. Just before she passed away my mom told me, "Expect a miracle, my life has been one." So when I am not feeling a deep sense of gratitude and I don't understand, I do my best to suspend my disbelief that love will find its way in my life. I am learning to have faith in endings — the title of this beautiful poem by Rebecca Braden.[24]

Faith in Endings

Sometimes in winter...

It happens
in hushed moments
just before the sun
descends behind
hazy mountain shadows.

...A slender veil of
otherness
mists in first.

A shy and hesitant
introduction
to nighttime.

...A kind of
quiet grieving
for what must end
for the day

you know
will never
ever
make an appearance
again.

An uncertain sigh
a reluctant farewell
a transient mention
of gratefulness
for all this day
has held.

Then the darkness
makes its
inexorable entrance
and the silent conversation
begins.

The one that tiptoes in
between
good-bye and hello.

The secret one . . .
spoken in the sanctuary
of your aloneness.

. . . Possibilities
before now
formless
begin to take form
there

in the darkness
in that silent conversation
in the stillness
in between.

. . . You have been invited.

You are welcome.

The joy of New Beginning . . .

. . . Dare your own
arrival, then.

Walk on
courageously
steadfastly . . .
hand in hand with Wonder. . . .

—Rebecca Braden

Deborah Welch, Christa Williams, and Ginny Gilmore

Creating Your Personal Journey

Thoughts from DUANE TRAMMELL

MANY ASTONISHING THINGS HAPPENED after Ginny's time in the woods of Door County . . . completing a degree program, establishing the Center for Spirituality and Leadership, creating the Sophia Foundation, and now eldering to many on their own journeys. This may raise many questions for you. You could be thinking, "I don't have the means or ability to drop everything and take a two-month sabbatical to figure out my next steps in life."

131

...I needed to find
a way to take a sabbatical
without really
taking a sabbatical.

While I was captivated and inspired by Ginny's process, I knew that I couldn't go away for that length of time. With my business partner's brain cancer advancing, she was unable to do any of the work we had shared for those many years. And our company finances were not in a place to hire another business partner of Ann McGee-Cooper's talent and reputation. Everything fell to me and my other presentation partner, Luis. Timm, our graphic designer, pitched in and helped with program planning. Carol on our team did double duty also, initially serving as Ann's personal assistant, but now adding hospital visits to her responsibilities. To keep our business afloat, there wasn't time for a sabbatical. There were even more hours added to the normally full workday. But as I read about Ginny's experience, I knew that I needed to find a way to take a sabbatical without taking a sabbatical.

First on my list was to read "The Healing Journey" again and begin to underline and mark practices and techniques Ginny employed while being alone in the cabin. I thought that if I could carve out thirty minutes or an hour each day, I could employ some of the practices during our company's transition and discover new insights.

At first, I identified twenty practices and wrote to Ginny about them:

Ginny,

Tonight I was drawn back into "The Healing Journey." You asked me in one of your messages to share what I was learning from it. I wasn't ready at that time. I needed to ponder it, live with it, and meditate on it. I will continue to do that. But I would like to share some first impressions.

I think what I needed most at this time was to see a picture of what it looks like to be confronted with big life changes and how to take a journey of exploration and find your inner voice. So, you can imagine how perfect your timing was for sharing this important part of your early journey. In the language of Christianity, this would be God reaching through you to me and showing me a way. And I even found it interesting that the book you were attracted to in this epic was Woman: Image of the Holy Spirit.

But I can also see the quantum physics of implicate order . . . the energy of your wisdom connecting to my need. Of course, it matters not how, but that your story found its way to me. And, it seems to be like an inner-work roadmap for me.

I wonder if you will find it odd that "The Healing Journey" spoke to me as a rather linear process. As I think about it, it isn't surprising . . . that is how I, Duane, understand and make sense of things . . . with lists and steps. I find it interesting that this was a very nonlinear experience for you. You set out with no spiritual roadmap . . . but intuited the process and lived in the moment with its twists and turns. But as you wrote it all down after the fact . . . the process emerges. Here's my "analysis":

1. Acknowledging and naming the passage and rite of change. A first step. I am there. I can feel it. I can sense it. It is scary. It is what I have shared with you in our first messages. I don't feel ready spiritually for the big changes that I know are going to be occurring in the next couple of years. I don't feel like I have a steady enough grounding. My knees get weak. But I felt your uncertainty in your story as your world changed. It was comforting to know you felt this, too.

2. A weekend retreat was a starting point. A sabbatical seems impossible to me. Two weeks away seems undoable at this point. But a two- or three-day introspection seems workable. Your story of the beginning of your journey was comforting. Because, I thought, "I can do this." I loved the weekend retreat story. Although, I will confess . . . I am not a camping kind of guy. I can honor and appreciate the beauty of nature, which I will . . . but I will sleep indoors (you will probably chuckle at this). The significance of the weekend was that it was a starting point that kicked things off for you.

3. Setting intention. After you decided that you would take a sabbatical solo and do this work, all matter of resources found their way to you. That is a good lesson. I loved the story of finding the rental. These are the kind of details that sometimes don't get written about in spiritual journeys. I love the practical side of your writing that fills in the details of how it happens as well as the big stuff that reveals itself.

4. A Mythical symbol reveals itself to you. I loved your story of Persephone. What this revealed to me was that ancient wisdom and ancient story-telling lives through the ages and becomes OUR story. I have to find my own hero. I have to find my own symbol of power. This is yet to be done. But it is an important part of the process.

5. Preparation. Your art workshop was an interesting piece of this process. That is the place where I am now. I feel like there are basic inner-work disciplines that I need to have as habits in order to make the most of my time when I do have a time of concentrated focus. Right now, I am getting up an hour earlier each day (something I thought I could never do and be at work on time at 8:00 a.m.) and I am walking and meditating for forty-five minutes. It is mostly dark, but I do manage to see the first lights of dawn. I have bought some wonderful instrumental orchestral tapes of favorite hymns. There is something about hymns that grounds me. My grandmother was a big part of my life and lived with us until I was twelve. I sense this connection, and although most organized religion has failed the world, there is a part of the inclusive message of progressive Christianity that I still have hope for. This morning time is helping me to find that same place of meditation during the daytime hours . . . and as I am understanding meditation practices . . . that is a goal.

6. Gratitude for the seasonal Earth. The season of fall played a significant role in your story. I loved the images you painted. I loved the meaning you ascribed to seasonal changes. I loved the metaphors. I find it interesting that we connected during the season of fall. If we were writing this movie, it couldn't have played out any more perfectly. I do know that my work will extend through the winter and perhaps even the spring. But the lesson that I learned from you is to honor the changes that the Earth shows us. The winter will teach me. And the spring will be a time of rebirth.

7. Ritual and routine hold the structure of exploring difficult changes together. Once again, my natural tendency shows here. Of course, I loved the part where you talked about establishing rituals and routines to make a structure of dealing with the days. The act of peeling fruit, juicing. I am examining daily rituals to recognize and honor in my life. The familiar will create comfort for the unfamiliar.

8. Wrestling with God. I loved this section of your writing. I have been doing that for the past nine months. I questioned my faith. I questioned my church attendance. I questioned all of it. I will always have questions. When I was about ready to give it up for a while, an amazing, charismatic, progressive, visionary, loving, electric, spiritual, ecumenical pastor entered the scene for our church. I love listening to Reverend Dr. Neil Thomas, spending time and finding spiritual meaning with him. He is countercultural with his spiritual invitation ... inviting atheists, agnostics, anyone, anywhere on their spiritual journey to be a part of our church community. That caught my attention. So ... I have a great dual journey going on—the outward one, along with this inward one that I am starting on.

9. Journey to the past. Processing memories. Honoring sacred wounds. Acknowledging major losses and major changes. This is some work that I will do. I know there is stuff there. So much happened with the illnesses and deaths of my parents, the death of my brother, a first failed relationship, and more. . . .

10. *The Artists Way* . . . free journaling. I intend on doing this. And in some ways, my writing to you is this. I find myself not withholding anything and freely writing to you, and you receive and are okay with that. I also remember so many good activities from that book to help get through to parts of me to find that inner voice and give it words.

11. Opening. Being sensitive to the present. When we open, you remarked that everything takes on a more brilliant color. You start noticing. I am even beginning to become aware of that now. On one of my morning walks I noticed seedpods in a tree in the park that I had never seen before. They were beautiful.

12. Even TV shows can have meaning. I absolutely loved the story of your waking up and turning on the TV to a movie that had a love story in it. It took on significant meaning to you. You sobbed. The story touched your heart and it was one of the catalysts for noticing the messages of the heart and the significance it would play in listening to your inner voice.

13. Creating a word journal. Yes. I will.

14. Reflecting on past other big changes and survival. I liked this as a separate activity. It takes some of the earlier work to be able to get to this point. But how valuable to recall and add meaning to the passages in our lives.

15. Paying attention to books you are attracted to. *Woman: Image of the Holy Spirit.* The inspiration and teaching this had for you. As you can tell, *Source: The Inner Path of Knowledge Creation*[25] is my book that started all of this. It continues to be monumental in this journey for me.

16. Honoring emotions. I learned from the story about this. You painted a clear picture of how to experience this and do this. I am basically a content and happy person. I don't handle negative emotions too well. I am learning to ask questions and seek help when I fear aspects of the future and not fear being afraid. And I know that inner work requires feeling some negative stuff as well as the joy.

17. Walking regularly around sunset. In addition to the mornings, I sometimes get an evening walk in. I like this time of day. I especially enjoy meditating in the park, watching the sun go down, and renewing. I found it gratifying to read about your walks in "The Healing Journey."

18. There may be "small anxiety attacks." Strangely enough, this was comforting. Mainly because I have experienced a few this year as some of these changes are occurring. There are some presentations that were difficult that I had to do without Ann for the first time in thirty years. My confidence waned. I felt like I didn't have what it takes to offer the credibility on my own. After the fact, the presentations were extremely successful. But that anxious feeling even made me sweat and be on the verge of throwing up. Yes. They are very real.

19. Make the experience Holy. I loved your references to this in HJ. This speaks to my heart and what I am feeling. I know that this is a Sacred, Holy Journey. I feel that in our relationship. It is countercultural. But I am learning to give honor and reverence to even preparing for the journey.

20. Do the inner work, and IT WILL BE REVEALED.
I thought the ending of "The Healing Journey" was brilliant. You will chuckle. I just knew that I was going to turn the pages in the last chapter and you would reveal what the meaning of life was and what your newfound calling would be. While there were clues and glimpses, you really shared that the Ending of your sabbatical solo was the just the Beginning . . . and as you committed to keep doing this inner work that in due time, the path would become clear . . . it would be revealed. This was the best lesson for me. And, I know it is what I will discover, too.

So . . . sorry this is so long. But ask and you will receive. This is what your story means to me. And . . . as I embark on each of these twenty insights and steps in the journey, I will go back, reread and relive your part of the journey as a fellow time traveler. While it has been twenty years ago for you, your journey becomes the present for me. That is the timelessness of the sacred.

Warmest hugs,
Duane   *October 2015*

Writing this chapter forty-eight months later, these practices didn't happen in order for me, and I learned quickly that inner work is not a linear process. On some days, I found myself practicing what came as number 12 for Ginny; other days I tried number 4 and nothing happened for me.

A Failed Attempt

Perhaps the funniest experience was when I attempted to do my "solo" experience in the woods. I felt like I needed to commune with nature like Ginny did. First, it is important to know that I live in the middle of downtown Dallas in a high-rise on the 25th floor. The closest I get to nature each day is walking through the manicured park in front of our condo building. The second thing to know is that camping is not my thing. But in the spirit of wanting to learn from nature and to listen deeply without the distractions of city life, I was determined to have a nature experience.

Granted, my timing was not great, but it was all I had. On a triple-digit day in Dallas's July heat, I packed my day-camping supplies and headed for nearby urban White Rock Lake. I found a secluded spot and set up camp. I had books and my journal and waited for the revelations from "on high" to come. I did thoroughly enjoy the sunrise. But soon the mosquitoes and other bugs came. It got unbearably sticky hot, no breeze, and even in the shade, the temperature soared. No matter how much I "meditated" all I kept thinking was how much more comfortable I would be in my high-rise condo in the air conditioning. After four hours, I surrendered, headed back, and took a nice cool shower. But it was a great lesson.

What I learned from this experience is that we have to create our own way of listening and finding our inner teacher. For some, it may be a wilderness adventure, for others of us, it may be a quiet space in our home where we hear the messages we need.

After exploring these practices for many months (for Ginny, years), we have found these to be the most helpful in navigating the choppy waters of major life transitions. Great authors have written about these practices, too:

- Meditation/prayer

- Mindfulness

- Reflection and journaling

- Inspiring reading

- Walks

- Email messages to a learning partner, sharing learning

- Spiritual time (for some, church)

- Time with friends to ponder

- Coaches to give feedback and explore with

A Better Attempt

Sometimes, providence creates a situation that enables taking time to do a healing journey experience. It so happened that in December 2018, we did not have any workshops or presentations on the calendar. At first glance at the schedule, I gulped. No presentations also meant no revenue coming in. While there was some billable coaching work and a whole lot of non-billable program writing I needed to do, this thirty-one-day block of available time got my attention. I felt called to take the spiritual sabbatical that I had envisioned three years earlier. Honestly, I don't think I was ready, but at this point, it was as if I had no choice . . . my heart was telling me "do this now!"

There were certain feelings and opportunities that I interpreted as "signs" that this could be a rich time of personal reflection and growth. Ginny had suggested we do an Advent study together using a wonderful book by Joyce Rupp, *The Star in My Heart*. And there was a special small-group Advent class at my church, Cathedral of Hope. It was being facilitated by Dr. Pat Saxton, a gifted teacher, who used contemplative practices to examine what was speaking to us. Although I moved in and out of work tasks occasionally, the major portion of the time was discretionary, and I could control how I used it.

Advent became even more than I had envisioned. Key insights jumped out at me. Connections with Matt Kosec spoke to me surrounding a vision for the future. Ideas about necessary endings in my life emerged. My body, mind, heart, and spirit slowed down enough so that I could finally hear messages I needed to hear. In the past, I could read the words "contemplative practices," "mindfulness," and "being present," but it was difficult to integrate in a daily schedule when the next deadline was screaming at me. For me, it required a longer period of uninterrupted time to quiet all the anxious chatter.

Ginny and I wrote to each other almost daily from our readings. I soaked in the work we did in our Advent class. Holiday parties surrounded this time, and it added to the joy of living in this sabbatical state. I found deeper connections and more interesting conversations at the events we attended. A culminating experience was volunteering for a Christmas event for clients of AIN (Access and Information Network) . . . a meal, party, and gift bags for those in need, many of whom were homeless. One middle-aged man, with striking good looks, graying hair at the temples, and a great smile, asked if there were a pair of jeans or slacks he could have. He had been living at a shelter for seven months. He was articulate, well-spoken, and if he had been in a $1000 suit, you would have mistaken him for a Fortune 500 executive. Yet, he was struggling to live and was grateful for the services provided by AIN.

You might ask, so what? What was the result of taking thirty-one days to step away, slow down, contemplate, journal, "be" in a different physical, emotional, intellectual, and spiritual place?

For me, it calmed some of the fears I had about the future. While there is still uncertainty, it quieted the voice telling me that the clock is ticking and business needs to come through the door soon. While there is truth to those words, obsessive worrying and over-attention produces anxiety that freezes the spirit and creativity.

I cannot adequately explain how contemplative practices help neutralize these fears, but they do. And there is another interesting realization: If what I am doing does not work, then it is not the end of the world. There will be something new to take its place. Change is not to be feared. Change is not failure. Change can open doors to a new opportunity.

What is the benefit of these practices during transition?

First, by listening, I had to identify my fears about this time of transition, and trust me, there were many:

• Fear of performing poorly and not being as capable as my business partner

- Fear of no new business coming in

- Fear of financial insecurity

- Fear of uncertainty in general — not knowing what would happen in the future

Fears can overwhelm you. I highly suggest securing a professional coach. I had several — a spiritual coach and other organizational mentors. Talking out your fears can make them less powerful. Some fears are there for a purpose, to move us to action. Other fears hang on because of old scripts we have playing in our heads. During times of transition, learning to sort these out is essential.

Second, I found that establishing practices like meditation, journaling, walking, reading, and reflecting ground us. It gives us a better foundation for not simply reacting to the changes. When we are able to slow down and respond, we do it with much better clarity of thought and ease.

Third, I'm learning that it is very easy to get caught up in my to-do list and put these great daily practices on hold — "I'll get to these later." I wish that I were more spiritually disciplined, but my tendency is to jump in and start tackling tasks. I have visual reminders on my desk to slow down and use these spiritual practices as a resource during my day. I still don't get a grade of A, but I am working my way up to a B-minus.

One caveat I would add. I am a disciplined person, yet I find it hard some days to stick to a rigorous schedule of spiritual practices. For months, I belittled and scolded myself about this until I read something from a book Ginny mentioned by Parker Palmer, *On the Brink of Everything: Grace, Gravity, and Getting Old.*

Duane volunteering in the kitchen at AIN

Duane and Steven at AIN's 2019 Art + Fashion + Community fundraiser

Parker quotes Thomas Merton: "It seems to me that I have greater peace . . . when I am not 'trying to be contemplative' or trying to be anything special, but simply orienting my life fully and completely towards what seems to be required of a man like me at a time like this." Parker goes on to say, "Simple and true, that, but so easily lost in Type A spiritual striving. What was required of me this morning was simply to make breakfast, despite my well-documented ineptitude. The deal is to do whatever's needful and within reach, no matter how ordinary or whether I'm likely to do it well."[26]

Your Personal Roadmap

It can be overwhelming when faced with a major life change. We have offered many ideas from our journeys. But finding a way to start can be half the problem. Here is a short list to consider. Have fun developing your own personal roadmap.

1. Acknowledge or name the transition you are in. Life has shifted. It has become different. Speak of it to others and honor it.

2. Set an intention to do inner work. Whether it is a two-month sabbatical or setting aside a part of each day for YOU.

3. Dedicate yourself to learning. Read, attend a class, join or create a discussion group.

4. Practice new, inner-work disciplines, listed on page 140. Through these practices your inner voice will speak to you. It will guide you through the time of transition.

5. Find a learning partner to be a reflective sounding board —
   a supporter and encourager of your process. Make it
   mutual — give and receive.

Duane and Ginny breaking bread

Growing Forward

Thoughts from VIRGINA GILMORE

MUCH HAS HAPPENED IN THE TWENTY-three years after going "into the woods." There were many wonderful things and some significant challenges as well. The time I spent in the woods opened a pathway for my life and how I might share with others how to live from the wisdom of our hearts. What I learned through my experiences in "The Healing Journey" served as a template for me to follow during times of unexpected difficulties and change. There were many people I met during these years who inspired me and who became important learning partners during this "second half of my life."

Transitions are wonderfully challenging and complicated.

You don't wrap up everything with a beautiful bow and call it "finished" after spending two months in the woods on a soul-searching sabbatical. Many aspects of your life come to light that need further work and exploration. Fortunately, I found Meredith Whelan, a gifted and talented therapist.

Meredith was my therapist during my time in the woods and for the next fifteen years of my life, helping me to make sense of my journey. The first time I met with Meredith I learned that she had completed Jean Houston's Mystery School program right before I went. It was uncanny how that happened. That's how I knew she was the "right person." As a therapist, she was spiritual and listened with the presence of generativity—helping me see new beginnings, new possibilities. My continuing journey into wholeness was hugely supported by Meredith. Having a good therapist can be crucial during difficult transitions. Meredith was both a therapist *and* spiritual director for me during those years. People have all kinds of feelings and ideas about "therapy." My experience with Meredith was one of the major ways I nurtured my own heart and soul. I am forever grateful to her. Meredith kept encouraging me to write a book, and one of my dreams is to give this book to her personally.

Marian University

"The Healing Journey" experience happened as a result of my bold idea to create a unique kind of leadership study under Gary Boelhower, then Vice President for Academic Affairs at Marian College (the name was changed to Marian University in 2008). I arrived at Gary's office late one summer afternoon in 1996 and explained that I wanted to complete my bachelor's degree by studying servant leadership and spirituality, which would include a two-month retreat in Door County. He listened with keen interest and agreed to support my request, directing me to Michael Ketterhagen, who would be my advisor and help design this study. I went straight to Michael's office, introduced myself, and then brought him up to speed on the plan. He was very open to being my advisor for this study. He was also receptive to my idea of a two-month retreat in the woods. Before I left his office, we had named this retreat "The Heroine's Journey" (later changed to "The Healing Journey"), my first class in this self-designed major, Spirituality and Leadership. Michael asked that I write a paper about the experience by the end of the semester.

The Center for Spirituality and Leadership

The experience of my time in the woods changed my life. It became the foundation for the rest of my life.

I completed my undergraduate work in December of 1998. One of the most meaningful experiences was the opportunity to work with Jack Christ, a professor of leadership from Ripon College, in a project designed to explore the "spirit" of leadership through interviews with leaders in organizations dedicated to servant leadership. With the help of Jack's video production company, our team of six traveled to three major organizations where we conducted videotaped interviews. Our goal was to learn more about servant leadership through their stories and experiences. These personal and organizational stories of success were very impactful to the servant leadership movement and are still shared today. Jack continues to be an enthusiastic learning partner and supporter of servant leadership.

After completing my degree, Gary Boelhower and I co-created the Center for Spirituality and Leadership at Marian University in October 2001. In preparation, I invited Richard Smith and Don Frick from the Robert K. Greenleaf Center for Servant Leadership to join Gary, Michael Ketterhagen, and Jack Christ, along with four other practitioners of servant leadership and myself, in a learning community we called the "Core Group." We agreed to do the work of learning, risking, and planning to form community with the purpose of birthing our shared vision. Our desire was to experience spirituality and leadership as individuals and as a community before creating a program or curriculum. We were committed to "be" in a learning community for two years before we would determine what we wanted to "do" with our learning.

In the fall of 2000, Gary Boelhower became the chair of the Virginia L. Duncan Professorship of Spirituality and Leadership, named after Ginny. From our Core Group learning experience, as well as consultation with some of the more prominent researchers, writers, and thought leaders in the country, the Center for Spirituality and Leadership was birthed in 2001. The curriculum Gary developed included components of the inner journey, servant leadership, dialogue, compassionate listening, systems thinking, and living from our "calling." Our conferences invited people from outside the university to learn about this radically different way of leadership practice and development. Gary created a two-year Institute for Authentic Leadership to attract executives to learn and grow together.

Challenging Leadership = Challenging Funding

Gary and I worked together for three years, sharing the main leadership experiences and challenges. Our decisions were made by dialoguing together, exploring all possibilities. We knew we were breaking ground in leadership development in ways that challenged the top-down leadership model. As a result, funding for the future of the program beyond the first three years was difficult. Ultimately, we had to accept that additional funding was not available for the continuation of the chair. Gary wisely suggested that the best step forward was to design a values-based leadership course that would bridge our work into the future. This course is still part of the curriculum at Marian University today.

After his outstanding work as the chair of the Virginia L. Duncan Center for Spirituality and Leadership ended, Gary made the decision to leave the university and move to Minnesota. Fortunately, Gary's experience provided a strong base from which he would continue to grow and serve. One of the many gifts since the move is his book *Choosing Wisely*. In it, Gary references the Heroine's Journey project and writes about the important work we did together over the years.

Endings and Heartbreak

When the Center for Spirituality and Leadership ended my heart was broken. It was an unexpected closure for me. I wondered if I had really heard God's calling when I helped create it. I questioned whether I had erred in how I stewarded the funds I had given to this vision. I found myself waking up in the middle of the night with doubts, unable to sleep, feeling piercing fear about how I had failed. It was a deeply frightening and lonely time. In the same way I "wrestled with God" during my healing journey, I had doubts about this ending. I stayed in this place for a couple of months, not listening to people who tried so hard to help me. Finally, through journaling, once again I found my way.

An Inspired Visit

One morning while journaling, I felt a strong need to see Parker Palmer, someone who has inspired me through his books and his life. This stunned me, and I decided to email Parker, telling him about my journaling breakthrough. He responded immediately, inviting me to his home two hours away in Madison, Wisconsin.

It was no mistake that my journal writing led me to Parker, who was a friend and mentor. He listened to me for over an hour with an attention that was totally present. Finally, he spoke. He told a story about a man he knew who had invested his heart and a great deal of money (at least ten times as much as I had) in a cause he cared about deeply. The event he financed didn't work out and that eventually led to the organization he had started ending its important work. Because this story was so close to my own, my heart filled with compassion for this man. Then Parker said, "I knew he was healing when I heard him speak almost five years later, and his talk had such a strong sense of humor." That was all he said. It was enough. Everything in me changed through the power of identifying with this story. I heard the connection between healing and humor, and my energy shifted very quickly. At that point, I started to talk about what we might create next. I left Parker's house with that sparkle back in my eyes again. I had just experienced the healing that can happen when someone is really present with another person. I was back on my feet again, ready to go forward, grateful beyond words. Little did I know that the work I'd done with Gary and Marian University was seeded in a way that would grow . . . just differently than I had expected it to.

Unexpected Honor

When Gary and I helped to form the Center for Spirituality and Leadership, we had a vision of how we thought it would grow. Gary worked tirelessly every day as the chair of this center. He continued to research and learn. He created curriculum for people to see leadership in a new way, the way of servant leadership. He wrote articles that got published locally and nationally. Many aspects of the learning process were rooted in what Gary did. When our work ended after three years due to lack of funding, my grief arose from believing that our efforts had been in vain and that this work was lost. My heart was also saddened by the loss of this dream with Marian University; the relationship that we shared in that dream was gone.

To my surprise, two years later in 2006, I received a call from Marian University informing me that I had been selected to receive the George Becker Spirit of Community Award at the annual business and industry dinner. This recognition lifted my heart. My family came to this event, almost filling a whole row in the auditorium. I will never forget Sister Mary Mollison handing me this award as I arrived on the stage. Our eyes met in a deep recognition of one another and the importance of the work of leadership and community. As I turned around to return to my seat, I realized that I was being given a standing ovation. I was stunned and deeply humbled. Healing was taking place in my heart, and the connection that I shared with Marian was being watered in ways that would allow it to grow.

On May 16, 2009, Mary Mollison called and invited me to give the commencement address for Marian University, announcing that I would be awarded an Honorary Doctorate of Humane Letters. Once again, as she "hooded me" and shook my hand, our eyes met. This time the joy in her spirit was overflowing. I believe that Mary midwifed something greater than herself when she helped our relationship heal and grow anew. What we started at Marian in 2002 was not lost at all. In fact, those seeds we planted were growing into strong plants of possibility, now "blessed" by the university itself!

The Sophia Foundation

What I learned at Marian gave me a passion to share it with others after my time there was done. My path was enlightened one day in a workshop entitled "Servant Leadership and the Personal Journey," led by Richard Smith. Richard conducted an exercise that greatly impacted me. He asked us to think of a time of success in our lives. I thought of my years with our family business, Kaytee Products. We were asked then to name an archetype of the energy of that experience for us. I immediately thought of Athena. Being in the corporate sales world was hard. It felt like it took an Athena-like spirit to succeed. Then Richard asked us to envision our future. What archetype would assist us to live there? Of course, I thought about Persephone, my friend in my time in the woods. But now who would accompany me into the vision of leadership and wisdom? I couldn't get the answer even though I felt the energy of it. Finally, three hours later, it came to me like a bolt of lightning. I blurted out, "It's Sophia," unintentionally disturbing the entire flow of the class. Richard, our facilitator, understood immediately and honored my "claiming." Sophia was my archetypal partner now!

Why Sophia? From the Greek, "sophia" is the word for wisdom. For many people it means Divine Feminine. In her book *The Star in My Heart*, Joyce Rupp shares, "Holy wisdom enters in unexpected ways, at unforeseen opportunities. All we have to do is keep the heart and mind available for her transforming movement. It has been my experience through the years that she brings us what is essential for our personal growth."[27]

Sophia conveyed our reaching into our hearts, finding our own wisdom, something that my healing journey gave me a chance to experience. My archetypes have always been feminine—Athena, Mary, Persephone, and Sophia (as Divine Feminine).

After reflecting on Sophia and what I felt was calling me now, I was encouraged by good advisors and willing partners to form the Sophia Foundation in 2002. Its purpose was to serve in ways that "fostered systemic change toward healing and wholeness, providing opportunities for learning and leadership that would enable human beings to become more caring people in leadership to each other." With the help of the Fond du Lac Area Community Foundation, a 501c3 charitable organization was formed—the Sophia Foundation—governed by a board of directors. In 2004, the board developed a vision (creating caring community), a mission (nurturing the spirit, dignity and potential of all people through transformative compassionate leadership), values, and operating principles to guide its work.

Until 2010, the Sophia Foundation primarily sponsored annual grants totaling more than $500,000 to support: (1) women and children in vulnerable situations such as abuse, illiteracy, home-lessness, and addiction; (2) leadership programs such as servant leadership and learning circles; and (3) broader community collaboration efforts like "Opening of the Heart," to support compassionate listening practices, and a community response against violence program called, "See It, Stop It, Change It— Violence Hurts Us All." In April 2005, Sophia gave a significant grant to the Fond du Lac Area Women's Fund to support the growth and well-being of women and girls in our community. As one of the founders of the Women's Fund, this gift was important to me, and I was grateful that Sophia could support this vitally important work. Sophia was able then to concentrate its focus on the potential of servant leadership within community.

Strategic Shift

In 2009, Sophia invested in two important programs and community-building initiatives. First, through the board members' generosity and expertise, Sophia began a leadership development program based on the principles and practices of servant leadership for nonprofit directors. Second, Sophia introduced the greater Fond du Lac area to servant leadership by hosting a community learning event, featuring Howard Behar, former president of Starbucks International. Howard ignited a strong interest in servant leadership for more than 200 community leaders in attendance through sharing his own leadership story.

Those two efforts helped the Sophia board realize that it could have greater impact as a community resource, teaching servant leadership skills and practices and influencing transformative change. In 2010, the board approved a strategy to shift from grant giving to the creation of direct programming related to servant leadership as the primary mission goal. Direct programming takes place when an organization delivers the programs itself rather than giving a grant to another agency to present the programming.

The board believed that this direction would have the best impact on transformation and systemic change. Since that time Sophia has created a number of leadership development programs and services that support individuals, teams, and organizations locally, regionally, and nationally to practice servant leadership.

I served as the founder and president of Sophia for fifteen years. It was the most challenging and rewarding experience of my life. My two children served on the board for the first ten years. Each made significant contributions, and we learned individually and as a family how to practice the Sophia operating principles, particularly dialogue. Now my children are making a difference in their own lives, drawing on their Sophia experience. Several people who participated in the Marian leadership work brought their learning to Sophia as founding board members, nurturing the dream and enabling the seeds that were planted there to continue to grow.

Gary Boelhower, my working and learning partner at Marian University, agreed to be a founding board member and served for thirteen years. His knowledge from the work we did at Marian was essential as we created our vision, mission, values, and operating principles, and held ourselves accountable to them. The wisdom gained from the Marian experience inspired our board to work together as a learning organization and as a "council of equals," making decisions by consensus. Gary ensured that these core principles guiding how we met, worked together, and made decisions were documented as "Guidelines for Sophia," still followed by the organization today. I will be forever grateful to Gary, the founding board members, and to all those who have served since.

My greatest growth in leadership evolved through my partnership with Christa Williams, Sophia's executive director. I shared my experiences, my library, teachers, and colleagues with Christa and the organization. We had an excellent coach, Deborah Welch, who guided us as we discovered our strengths and how best to support one another in our work with the organization and with those we served. We developed a generative relationship that I consider a lifetime gift. It was a very productive time for Sophia and a very fulfilling time for me.

Winds of Change

As I was nearing the age of seventy, I had a life-changing experience that contributed to the decision to conclude my time with Sophia. I was once again being invited to a new chapter in my life. I had confidence that Christa was ready for this change, and we worked together with the organization on a three-year transition plan. On December 21, 2016, my husband Jim and I retired from the Sophia board. An important part of this transition process was my deep yearning for the work of Sophia to be sustained. I knew that it would take dedicated leadership to make this happen. I sensed a new calling and realized that Sophia had a calling of its own. I had to let Sophia go with my blessing so that the people leading it forward had the freedom to do it their way.

In 2012, I had an interview with a mentor and friend, George SanFacon. He offered to translate our interview into a mind-map of images to help me see the "picture of my life." Our connection during the interview was generative. I reflected on how things had evolved from childhood (when I spent time in my treehouse), to Kaytee (our family business), to the retreat time in the woods (learning about the inner journey), to Marian (where I graduated with the calling to "radically change the way we teach and learn about leadership"), to Sophia (where the seeds planted would root and grow). George's questions tapped into a "knowing" inside me. I recounted my life stories and as I understood the meaning of each one, I began to see the interconnection between the stories and what was calling me now.

The Indian Elder Woman

During the call with George, I had a mystical kind of experience that has happened to me occasionally at key times in my life. An image just dropped in to my mind. It was an image of an Indian Elder Woman with a peace pipe. I told George what was happening. It changed the energy of our call. Up to that point, I had talked about how tired I was from all the years of leading Sophia and the work of servant leadership. The Indian Elder Woman opened up an entirely new dimension of our conversation.

Two weeks later, I received the mind map—the image story of my life—from George. I immediately knew that the Indian Elder Woman would show me a more reflective way to live and serve, where my energy would be restored and sustainable at this stage of my life. For a long time, I had been hearing the phrase "elder leader." Not completely sure of what it meant, I realized the Indian Elder Woman was pointing me in this direction. I needed to make some changes and let go of what I was doing now with Sophia. I knew it would be difficult and disruptive, but I had to act. I had to say "yes" to the calling I was hearing.

This revelation stunned me. After the initial shock, I told Christa that I had to leave Sophia. I described my interview with George, showed her the mind map, and shared that I needed to leave in the next six months. I felt what Abraham must have felt when he thought he was supposed to kill his son. The command was nonnegotiable, so he just moved toward it. My situation didn't come close to killing one's child, but in many ways, Sophia was like a child to me, and Christa was like family.

Hearing my words, Christa turned totally white. I can still feel the emotions of that moment. She felt like I was abandoning her. I felt like I was abandoning her. And thankfully, that "Voice" came through to let me know — let us both know — that this did not have to happen immediately. I was being shown the direction, not the destiny. The timing became much clearer as we began look at what would need to happen before my departure in order to give Sophia time to adjust and prepare. We developed a three-year plan, and Christa, the board of directors, and I began this transition which would invite Sophia and me to take different paths in our next season of growth!

During this three-year period, I remembered my time in the woods, and I was very intentional about the process of change. I read, journaled, walked, reached out to friends, and made sure I had my quiet reflective time every morning. I was so fortunate to find a spiritual director to work with me on a monthly basis. We never met in person, but our connection was very sacred, safe, and supportive. Ronna Detrick challenged me in ways that let me see myself more clearly. It was obvious from our sessions that this change was hard. It was not only about leaving the work I had known for the last twelve years; it was also about embracing what it meant to be an elder. Upon my retirement from Sophia, I would be seventy years old. Back in 1996, when I was in the woods, I knew I would leave from there and continue my education at the university. This time, I had no idea what was ahead. I needed Ronna's continual assurance that I would find new ways to serve with as much passion as I had before.

The three years of preparation were challenging and meaningful for me. At Sophia, I supported the first person to be president other than myself. I attended all the board meetings, practicing my role as an elder and advisor rather than president. Cathy Wolfe, a board member since Sophia began, joined Gary, Christa, and me as we explored the roots and heart of Sophia to document what we all hoped would be passed on as the organization continued to grow and change.

At the end of three years, I felt a sense of peace about all of these preparations. But I was exhausted, and had very little passion for any more work. A spiritual teacher who crossed my path pointed out that this is not unusual. There are "valley times" when we pull back to rest and renew that can last for two or three years. When I heard this I was relieved, and I relaxed more into the experience of waiting.

Ending with a Blessing

Much of my time on the calls with Ronna was focused on creating a blessing for Jim and me to offer to the people of Sophia during the final celebration. My spiritual direction sessions helped me to surrender my concerns, trusting that Sophia had what it needed and so did I.

On December 21, 2016, my husband Jim and I participated in a mutual ritual of blessing between the organization and us. We remembered and celebrated the fifteen years, acknowledging the highlights of our experience. It was sacred and beautiful. I felt pain in my heart as well as relief that the time for change had come. When Jim and I walked out of the room, I knew I was crossing a threshold into the next chapter of my life.

Eldering into the Future

As I left that night after the Sophia board celebration, I sensed the same energy boost that I felt when I drove out of Door County that late October day in 1996. Now, I was close to seventy years old. Twenty years had passed since the time in the woods. Yet the feelings were similar. This time I did not have a plan for my future. I was leaving the framework that held me so beautifully for fifteen years. But I had to go forward, trusting that the way would find me as it had before.

At this point in my life, I was happily married to Jim Gilmore, having just celebrated our twelfth anniversary. My children were happy and thriving with their spouses in New York and Chicago. Jim and I were blessed with four beautiful grandchildren, ages ten and under, and we enjoyed all the time we could with them. We had created homes for ourselves in Door County as well as Bonita Springs, Florida, in addition to our Fond du Lac home. Having moved to Florida three years earlier for the winter months, we were still developing our sense of community there. As we arrived in Florida shortly after the final blessing with Sophia something shifted. I was feeling drawn toward new ways to be and serve.

Many helpful, meaningful coincidences happened during this time. A stronger connection with Duane Trammell gave me a spiritual partner who was also going through a deep transition as he supported our mutual friend and his working partner of thirty-five years, Ann McGee-Cooper, in the final months of her journey with cancer. I sent Duane a copy of "The Healing Journey" so he could know me better. His response surprised me. It gave him helpful ideas about structuring his own time of transition. He wanted to work with me to publish it. That idea brought me energy and hope. Something else happened to affirm this possibility as well as to offer me additional ways to learn and grow.

One day while ordering a book from Amazon, another book showed up on my screen. It was entitled *Conscious Living, Conscious Aging*, by Ron Pevny. I immediately ordered the book. Later, as I began reading, it was clear that buying this book was no accident. The introduction says that this book offers "visions and approaches for older adults to live with more fulfillment, intention, and joy as they age."[28] Pevny writes about "meaning, passion, growth and service" in this time of eldering. He adds that "the role of the elder is archetypal."[29] His words piqued my interest. Pevny goes on to say, "The wisdom and gifts of elders have been universally valued as necessary for the emotional and spiritual health and balance of societies. This archetypal energy still seeks expression today amid the many powerful changes shaking the cultural landscape."[30] I knew this book was calling me; I had no doubt.

I read on, understanding more clearly why this book found me. In the chapter, "The Power of Story to Shape our Future," Pevny writes:

The work of recontextualizing our lives is greatly enhanced by remembering that as we enter life, we are all called to enact our unique version of the hero's journey. In doing so, we are living mythically. Jean Houston, along with Joseph Campbell and others, has done much to help the modern world understand the power of myth. She wrote that myth "is story invested with all of our potentials and highest ideals, as well as our shadows and terror. . . . It provides a template that allows us to open ourselves to the hidden capacities we had forgotten we had; the creative potentials we didn't know how to use; the deeper knowing that transcends past, present and future – a deeper knowing that is within every one of us. [31]

He goes on to say:

However, living in a modern world that has little understanding of the mythical dimension of life, we tend to see our lives as individual small stories with no inherent meaning, largely shaped by random events and experiences. If the world's myths do indeed point to inherent meaning in our human experience, and if the hero's journey is indeed the master myth – the soul's template for the human process of growth – then our passage through life can best be understood as a highly meaningful journey involving sorrow and joy, loneliness and community, endings and beginnings, experience and learning – all toward the fulfillment of our unique human potential. Conscious eldering is about choosing to intentionally embark on the final chapters of our hero's journey, entering unchartered territory to discover our potential to bring the gifts of true elders to a world urgently in need. Recontextualizing helps us recognize and acknowledge ourselves as the hero or heroine going on the journey into elderhood. We are on the lifelong larger journey of unfolding our own personal myth. [32]

Here it was again . . . was still very much alive in me as I began this new chapter in my life. No wonder that I noticed a similarity in my feelings upon leaving Sophia to when I drove away from Door County. It was a later stage of the same deep thread of my own life journey. Persephone had grown now into the Indian Elder Woman with the peace pipe. I began to better understand why the term "eldering" had been calling me.

I have always created circles of people with whom to learn. I wanted to read Pevny's book with others who were experiencing what I was. I sent it to Duane. I asked my good friends in Florida and Wisconsin to read it with me, and we formed four-week learning circles to discuss it together. I gifted this book to many people, and some of them formed learning circles of their own.

Before long, I was asked to help facilitate book studies at my church. This is something I have always loved doing. Forming teaching-learning communities was a calling that I had lived ever since my two years with Jean Houston. She had heard about these communities from her mentor and good friend Margaret Mead. Margaret Mead wanted Jean to "just create teaching-learning communities." I learned about this during Jean's Mystery School, and I have done it ever since.

"Grace, Gravity, and Getting Old"

More recently, another book that has helped define eldering for me is Parker Palmer's latest book, *On the Brink of Everything: Grace, Gravity, and Getting Old*. He invites us to consider: "Old age is no time to hunker down, unless disability demands it. Old is just another word for nothing left to lose, a time of life to take bigger risks on behalf of the common good." [33]

Parker goes on to teach us: "The laws of nature that dictate the sunset dictate our demise. But how we travel the arc between our own sunrise and sundown is ours to choose: Will it be denial, defiance, or collaboration? . . . This book, my tenth, is on the fruit of my collaboration with aging . . . an offering from a fellow traveler to those who share this road, pondering as they go." [34]

Parker shares his experience of aging and invites us to reflect on interesting, different aspects of aging: seeing from a broader perspective; partnering with younger generations; designing a new vocation by staying engaged with the world, and engaging with our souls until the end.

My Eldering Life

As I meet new people, I often enjoy lunch conversations with them. I find that we connect regarding our meaning, our spirituality, and the process of eldering. From these various connections, I have had an opportunity to serve as a spiritual guide for some. My eldering is finding form once again. I am surprised that some of these ties are flourishing with younger people — something that lights me up.

Sophia continues to grow and change. In 2018, Sophia Foundation changed its name to Sophia Transformative Leadership Partners to be more reflective of the work it does today. Sophia remains dedicated to its original operating principles, values, mission, and vision and is evolving to more clearly communicate the calling I heard in my heart upon graduating from Marian — now echoed in its approach, partnerships, programs, and services. Transformative leadership for Sophia involves facilitating a major change to someone or something that makes them, their lives, organizations, community, and world better.

The board has defined my role now as elder, and my title is "Wisdom Leader and Advisor." Christa and I share monthly phone calls in which I listen, ask questions, and offer appropriate input when relevant. I meet periodically with the officers of the organization to focus on new ways to learn about wisdom. I continue to introduce new people, books, and ideas to Christa and the board, as I have a renewed passion for learning. The continued development of Sophia's work and my role as elder gives me great joy.

The greatest joy comes from "creating caring community" with my husband and our family. My marriage of fifteen years to Jim Gilmore has truly been a gift of love in my life. We appreciate every day, and the ways we support one another give us joy. Time with our children and grandchildren is precious to us. We are learn-

Ginny with her husband, Jim Gilmore

ing to be a friend and mentor to them, to encourage them to follow their hearts, knowing their strengths and gifts, on their own "hero's journey."

Over the last four years, I have once again found expressions of my passion, and my desire to serve others is fully engaged. Many of the things that support my spiritual grounding came out of my time in the woods in Door County years back. These are essential to maintaining my capacity of awareness and presence. The two hours I spend each morning in quiet prayer, reflection, and journaling as a form of gratitude are vital to my spirit. Periodically during the year (such as the Lenten season), Duane and I share a book of reflections and our daily journaling with each other. Having a spiritual partner is very life-giving for both of us. Also, the continued opportunity to co-facilitate a Virtual Servant Leadership Learning Community® program is spiritually nourishing. In its tenth year, this program is for leaders who want to know more about servant leadership and their own inner journey. I am challenged to continue to learn about the practices

Ann McGee-Cooper and Ginny

of servant leadership that support ongoing healing and the capacity to better serve others in their work and life journeys. I look forward to experiencing more retreat time for myself and working with partners to design retreat experiences for others.

Ongoing Calling

What continues to "call" me is encouraging people as they navigate the transitions in their lives. I enjoy providing spiritual mentoring and support to those experiencing change, whether it be a young person going to college, a person at fifty wondering what that means, a person entering retirement, or a person who is noticing how different life looks as we enter our seventies. I love to help people understand what they most care about and then to watch the steps they take toward that goal.

I continue to wonder what the peace pipe means that the Indian Elder Woman had. Perhaps it relates to finding peace in one's self. I sense it is relational because that fits who I am. What I do know is that I am learning to access a deeper courage to step up where I may have been afraid before. I am learning to hold paradox in tension. This seems important now as an elder and for this time in our history. I continue to be a student today, as much as I have been in the past, and my passion to serve is strong. "What I know for sure," as Oprah says every month in her magazine, is that giving myself the gift of silence every day, and intentional retreat time on a regular basis, is essential for me to feel connected to the wisdom of my heart—a "knowing" that comes through the Sophia guides I have known through the years. If I hadn't paused my life in 1996 to go to the woods for those two life-changing months, I would not have discovered this. That time set me on a new path of serving others that has continued to grow ever since.

Robert Greenleaf has a wonderful quote which remains in my heart and spirit. In his essay "Old Age: The Ultimate Test of Spirit," he offers this: ". . . the ultimate test for spirit in one's old age is, I believe, can one look back at one's active life and achieve serenity from the knowledge that one has, according to one's lights, served? And can one regard one's present state, no matter how limited by age and health, as one of continuing to serve?" [35]

Being engaged in ways that serve others . . . that is and always will be an essential part of my life.

Ginny's family

Afterword

Duane's Final Thoughts

GINNY AND I STARTED WORK-
ING ON THE IDEA FOR THIS BOOK FOUR
years ago and thought we would have it
completed in a year. We learned that for
some projects, time is not linear. Experiences arose for each of us, and the book
began writing itself. Had we not experienced more losses, fears, successes, disappointments, failures, happiness, fulfillment, and meaning, we would not have
understood that the HJ process never
truly ends. It is a spiral . . . a circle that
repeats itself over and over again. And
the spiral can go up or down. It is our
choice.

For me, it is about learning to live in
paradox and ambiguity and accepting
that. I am slowly learning to live by faith
and reality at the same time. I can be anxious about programs or lack of contracts

and at the same time feel greatly fulfilled from the work we are doing. My surrender has been moving from security to the unknown. The HJ process helps me navigate the darkness.

I didn't like darkness as a child. It frightened me. My husband lived in southwestern Missouri in a remote, heavily wooded area where there was no light at night. It won't surprise you that we chose to live in the city center, downtown Dallas. We look out our windows and always see light, cars, and activity . . . even at 3:00 a.m. I find comfort in the words of Joyce Rupp, "In the darkest part of night, God has provided billions of stars as a reminder, that even in the darkest of times, there is light."[36] God has also provided cars, streetlights, and ambient lighting, too.

Change and transitional periods in our lives can be scary and a wonderful opportunity to pause, dig deeper, and find meaning. Whether your HJ experience is two months (like Ginny's time in the woods), two weeks, or two years, you can make it a rite of passage, exploring possibilities of growth and purpose.

As I write these words in 2019, another major business change has happened. A long-term client decided to shift training from Trammell McGee-Cooper and Associates (TMCA) to a new curriculum provided by another consulting firm. If this had occurred three years ago, I would have panicked. While the news was sad and sobering, this work in dealing with transitions has been greatly helpful. Even though the change is not something I would have chosen, it provided me the opportunity to reflect, problem solve, and consider a new and different life in 2020. Various possibilities began materializing—ones that I would not have considered had I not been thrust into change. I also realized I needed to balance hopefulness with the complexity of uncertain business consulting realities. If we are faithful to the process of listening, learning, working on ourselves, and being open . . . answers emerge.

Ginny's Final Thoughts

AFTER COMPLETING FIFTEEN YEARS IN LEADERSHIP with Sophia, I again experienced that time of wondering and waiting, not knowing what was next with my deep dedication to serve. When Duane wrote me that caring email in July 2015 after my neighbor's funeral, I had no idea that our connection would lead to this book. I am still astonished even now as I write. My heart leapt when his message came, suggesting that we collaborate to publish HJ because it had helped him so much. The opportunity to learn with Duane over these last four years has gifted my spirit more than I can say. We have shared our spiritual journeys through books that inspire us, particularly during Advent and Lent. We have listened deeply to one another's souls through exchanging our writings. We have mirrored back to one another, sharing what we hear, sometimes at a deep generative level, often accompanied by open questions. This book, I believe, has been inspired by this regular practice of writing to one another.

Duane and I continue to experience transitions. We continue to listen to and follow our hearts, not always knowing where they will lead us. We have learned that if we do this, the way will be shown to us. It may not be clear at first, but by supporting each other in ways that nurture our faithfulness, we each continue to experience our lives as meaningful and more fully alive.

This spring I had an unexpected experience. Christa invited me to share a presentation about Sophia in Phoenix with a group of dedicated leaders brought together by our friend Deborah, and some other colleagues and friends. Good things happened from that experience. We are now preparing to use that same presentation in a Sophia board retreat. I see this as fulfilling part of my calling as an elder—supporting Christa and others who are so courageously taking the work of Sophia forward. I treasure the beautiful people in my life who teach and inspire me every day with their courage, humility, and faithfulness to a life of meaning, love, and service. I give thanks for the many memorable moments of my life with my husband Jim as we celebrated our fifteenth wedding anniversary last October. I give heartfelt thanks for the opportunities I have to be with my children, their spouses, and my four grandchildren, the oldest of whom recently became a teenager. Every summer, our family gathers in Door County on the Fourth of July for a traditional holiday celebration. My daughter, her husband, and their children stay for a very active and happy month with Jim and me in our home on the water, not far from that little cottage in the woods where "The Healing Journey" began twenty-three years ago! The cycles continue. Where will Sophia take me next? All I know is that I will do my very best to continue to say "yes" to this journey we share together, perhaps understanding even more clearly where Sophia, now Indian Elder Woman with the peace pipe, will take me.

QUESTIONS
to go Deeper

For Individual Reflection or a Small Study Group

1. What transition or life-change are you in currently? How would you describe it? intellectually? emotionally? physically? spiritually?

2. What resonated with you the most reading Ginny's "The Healing Journey"? What could you identify with?

3. Through her journey, Ginny's energy guide was the Greek goddess Persephone. Who might be your metaphorical guide through your transition?

4. An amazing series of events landed Ginny in her cabin in the woods of Door County, Wisconsin. Do you have a favorite place to reflect? A vacation home, a nature site near your home, a favorite room, or a comfy chair in a quiet corner that could serve as a sacred space for reflection? What makes a place feel like "home"?

5. Developing a new appreciation for silence was important in Ginny's and Duane's journeys. Silence allows us to hear the sound of truth and connect to the soul. How do you feel about silence? How long are you comfortable with silence? How could you create times of silence for yourself? Ginny found silence in the woods. Duane found silence in the middle of the city. Where is your respite?

6. Many books have been written on forgiveness. Deborah Welch, one of the contributors to our book, wrote *Forgiveness at Work: Stories of the Power, Possibility, and Practice of Forgiveness in the Workplace*. Is "forgiveness work" a part of your journey? Self-forgiveness?

7. The woods had a special place in Ginny's heart from childhood. Is there a childhood place that holds a special place in your heart?

8. Facing fears is a part of the healing journey. What fears surround the transition you are dealing with? How can you face those fears and overcome them?

9. How do the seasons of the year speak to your life? How might each season be a metaphor or offer insight in addressing your transition?

10. Ginny and Duane have both experienced "calling" throughout their lives. Have you ever felt "guided"? What next steps seem possible following this transition?

11. If your transition concerns leaving or loss, how can you best say "goodbye"? How do you prepare to leave? How do you transform heartbreak into wholeheartedness?

12. Which books have made a difference in your life? What could you read now that would help you with the unexpected change?

13. Duane saw a "process" in Ginny's spiritual sabbatical in the woods and identified steps that could be applied to any transition. Where are you in your process? Which steps could help you grow through your own circumstances?

14. Steve Thiry went through a tragic event as a first responder. What key elements contributed to his healing that might work for you?

15. Matt Kosec's story involved every aspect of the healing journey ... successful career, a mistake, deep soul searching, vulnerability, shame, forgiveness, discovering what his soul really needed, and finding his true calling. What aspects of his story do you identify with? How are you listening to what your soul is seeking?

16. Deborah Welch's story focused on the importance of dreams. Do you remember your dreams? What are your dreams teaching you about the transition you are in?

17. Ginny used poetry to open each chapter of her original work. Which poem spoke to you the most? Why? How does it relate to your transition at this moment?

18. What is the next step to deal with the transition you are in?

> *If the changes and transitions in your life are painful*
> *and you find yourself struggling,*
> *we encourage you to seek professional help*
> *as the authors of this book did.*
> *You are not alone.*

With GRATITUDE

M ANY REMARKABLE PEOPLE
HELPED IN THE CREATION
OF THIS BOOK.

We would like to give special thanks to our amazing book team who were not only the best professionally skilled in the business, but who also took this manuscript into their hearts and souls; they translated our words into beautiful lyrics and intimate page designs. Thank you, Deborah Costenbader, for taking our words and filling them with clarity and understanding. Thank you, Suzanne Pustejovsky-Perry, for making each chapter of our book and the cover a work of art. Thank you, Timm Chamberlain, for the patience and technical skill to set the text and images to get us past the finish line to printing. This team has added life to this book in ways we never imagined. Working with them is to know what servant leadership looks like and feels like, always centered in what is the best experience for the reader. For that, we are forever grateful.

Thanks to our readers and proofers—Jenny Knuth, Sue Roettger, Luis Duran-Aparicio, Beth Seif, Carol Haddock, and Jim Gilmore. Your attention to detail helped us to have a more accurate book.

Thanks also to Jenny Knuth and Christa Williams for their excellent marketing partnership.

We want to thank our three guest authors, Steve Thiry, Deborah Welch, and Matt Kosec. They each read "The Healing Journey" and applied it to transitions in their lives. Their hope, and our hope, was that by hearing others' stories, it would help our readers know it is possible to heal from all kinds of tragedies.

Thank you, Ann McGee-Cooper, for connecting the two of us. While Ann lived, she taught us about the importance of spending quiet time in reflection before working in seminars. We felt your support from heaven through all of our writing process.

Thank you to so many mentors and teachers, like Ann, who have inspired our servant-leader journey in ways that have changed our lives. To each of you, thank you forever.

We each have people we would like to thank separately who inspired and supported us in our own lives and in the ideas shared in *Wisdom from the Woods*.

Ginny's Appreciations

In 1996, when I realized that there were three vital parts of my life that were radically changing, I knew I needed help. Taking the step to spend a weekend in Door County with my good friend Loretta was a life-changing decision. Because of that weekend, I was inspired to go to Marian College and talk with two professors about a focused study that would include a two-month retreat in the woods of Door County. Without the deep listening and support of both Dr. Gary Boelhower and Dr. Michael Ketterhagen, "The Healing Journey" would not have been written. I am grateful beyond words for all the ways they nurtured my journey as I earned my degree and in all the years since.

In the original manuscript of "The Healing Journey," Dr. Ketterhagen wrote, "This could be published." I never forgot that. It lay dormant in my library for many years before my insightful friend Duane read it and was inspired by it. He, too, told me that "this needs to be published." The time had come, and through Duane's shared gifts and partnership, this writing is now coming to you. I can never thank Duane enough for the many ways he has been a light in my life as a learning partner of the heart and soul.

From the time Duane and I started to turn the vision of this book into reality, my husband, Jim, has remained a constant encourager and supporter, a steady and deeply loved and appreciated member of the team. Jim is a beacon of love and light in every day of my life!

My time in the woods revealed to me the most precious gift of the time I spend with my children, Rob and Ginger. I am so grateful to them for the many ways we have continued to learn and grow together, including many times of unexpected challenges. The love and support for one another in our family is a blessing beyond measure.

Starting new organizations that are project-driven means that there is a need for many partnerships to support different aspects of the work. Beth Seif was the "behind the scenes" person who kept it all going with her work in the office in our home. She has been a deeply valued partner for the past twenty years and has provided a significant amount of the support needed for this book. She always worked with a smile and a spirit of perseverance — a vitally important part of the team that worked to make this book possible.

Christa Williams has been a learning partner and co-creative leader of the work of Sophia since she started in 2007. Her love and passion for the work as executive director of Sophia continue to inspire me and so many others. I am grateful for our heart connection which enables us to learn and grow together. I have deeply appreciated her input, encouragement, and support in many areas, including this book, during these last four years.

A deep thread of spiritual focus in my life has come from the sacred retreat time I have shared twice a year for more than twenty years with my "Dharma Sister," Deborah Welch. I will be forever grateful to Deborah for her friendship and inspiration, for her encouragement with this book, and for the many moments we have shared in the story it tells.

I started the healing journey with my dear friend Jean Miller. We shared many walks and talks during my time in Door County and for many years afterward. She taught me how to stop and notice the beauty of nature that I had missed when I was busy. Thank you, Jean, for sharing with me that you read "The Healing Journey" one more time just before you died. And thank you for being our angel while we have been preparing this book to go out into the world.

And to so many mentors, teachers, family, friends, and colleagues, who have been learning partners on this continuing journey of life, I say, "Thank you always, with love forever."

Duane's Appreciations

Ginny and I have had a dream of publishing a book together since our friendship deepened in September 2015. A remarkable relationship quickly developed between us, and we each knew that there was a purpose in our paths intersecting at one of the most vulnerable moments of our lives. Building on Ginny's original "Healing Journey" manuscript as a foundation, we conceived the idea of creating a longer book together, and *Wisdom from the Woods* began. We thought we could complete the book in one year, but it needed four and one-half years to be nurtured and born. And we understand why. We both needed the time to experience and learn from more transitions. Ginny has been a constant support, encourager, teacher, friend, and spiritual mentor in my life.

Thank you, Carol Haddock, who has been with me as a business partner and friend for twenty-five years. She helps me stay organized, skillfully handles details of my business, and was a reader and proofer for this book. Her friendship has seen me through times of grief, uncertainty, and celebrations.

Luis Duran-Aparicio inspires me with his positivity, presents programs with me, and faithfully practices the skills we teach in this book. He and I have long car trips traveling to client presentations during which we delve into the topics from *Wisdom from the Woods*.

He enlightens me with the perspective of a younger generation. Thank you also for serving as a reader and proofer for this book.

Matt Kosec has been a sustaining force in my life, helping me to understand and navigate the unexpected changes in life that have happened in the past four years. Matt and I meet regularly and share our hopes, dreams, disappointments, and care for one another.

During my own healing journey, I had a wonderful spiritual guide, Sally Metzger, who worked with me weekly, encouraging me, helping me talk to my subconscious, instilling confidence, and helping me to heal from the deep grief of losing Ann. I am so grateful for the encompassing love she showed me to help me move forward.

I am blessed to have a remarkable husband, Steven Pace, who continues to help the economically and physically disadvantaged in the scary and dangerous times of COVID-19 as this book process is nearing completion. Steven has been with me through dark days and bright days. He not only has encouraged and supported me through all of the transitions of our lives, but he also has given me inspiration, love, and encouragement during the writing of *Wisdom from the Woods*.

GINNY AND I BOTH WISH YOU WELL as you hear your own "wisdom from the woods" and navigate life's unexpected challenges.

MEET THE AUTHORS, WATCH VIDEOS AND MORE AT
WisdomfromtheWoodsBook.com

NOTES

1 Parker Palmer, *Let Your Life Speak: Listening for the Voice of Vocation* (San Francisco: John Wiley & Sons, Inc., 2000), 7.

2 Judith Duerk, *Circle of Stones* (San Diego: Lura Media, 1989), 29–30.

3 T.S. Eliot, "East Coker," *Four Quartets* (New York: Houghton Mifflin Harcourt, 1978), 16–17.

4 Jean Shinoda Bolen, *Goddesses in Everywoman* (New York: Harper & Row Publishers, Inc., 1985), 197.

5 Maureen Murdock, "Looking for the Lost Pieces of Myself," *The Heroine's Journey: Woman's Quest for Wholeness* (Boston: Shambhala Publications, Inc., 1990), 91–92.

6 Richard Rohr, "Days of Renewal" (Cincinnati: The Fountain Square Fools, circa 1995), cassette tape series and no longer available.

7 Virginia Duncan Gilmore, "Life Is about Listening" (Door County, WI, Personal Journal, September 1996).

8 Julia Cameron, *The Artist's Way* (New York, G.P. Putman's Sons, 1992), 9–18.

9 Cameron, *The Artist's Way*, 9–18.

10 Wendell Berry, "Sabbaths 1979, I," *This Day: Collected & New Sabbath Poems* (Berkeley: Counterpoint Press, 2013), 7.

11 Schaupp, *Woman: Image of the Holy Spirit* (New Jersey: Dimension Books, 1975), 19.

12 Schaupp, *Woman: Image of the Holy Spirit*, 17–24.

13 Schaupp, *Woman: Image of the Holy Spirit,* 108.

14 Thich Nhat Hanh, *Living Buddha, Living Christ* (New York: Riverhead Books, 1995), 14–15.

15 Rick Jarow, "The Seat of Prosperity," *Lotus Personal Transformation*, 6, no. 1 (1996): 79.

16 Hanh, *Living Buddha, Living Christ,* 37–38.

17 Hanh, *Living Buddha, Living Christ,* 38–39.

18 David Wagoner, *Traveling Light: Collected and New Poems* (Chicago: University of Illinois Press, 1999), 10.

19 Judith Barr, "Persephone — Come Back from the Underworld," *News of the Sacred Work of the Feminine* (Mysteries of Life), No. 5 (1996), 1–2.

20 Joyce Rupp, *The Star in My Heart* (Notre Dame, IN: Sorin Books, 2010), xxiv.

21 Robert Greenleaf, *The Servant as Leader* (Westfield, IN: The Robert K. Greenleaf Center, 2008), 29.

22 Jeremy Taylor, *The Wisdom of Your Dreams: Using Dreams to Tap into Your Unconscious and Transform Your Life* (New York: Penguin, 2009), 106–108.

23 Taylor, *The Wisdom of Your Dreams,* 106–108.

24 Rebecca Braden, "Faith in Endings," unpublished poem. (This poem has been shortened here.)

25 Jaworski, Joseph, *Source: The Inner Path of Knowledge Creation* (San Francisco: Berrett-Koehler Publishers, 2012).

26 Parker Palmer, *On the Brink of Everything: Grace, Gravity, and Getting Old* (Oakland, CA: Berrett-Koehler Publishers, Inc., 2018), 77.

27 Rupp, *The Star in My Heart,* ix.

28 Ron Pevny, *Conscious Living, Conscious Aging: Embrace & Savor Your Next Chapter* (New York: Atria, 2014), xv.

29 Pevny, *Conscious Living, Conscious Aging,* xix.

30 Pevny, *Conscious Living, Conscious Aging,* xix.

31 Pevny, *Conscious Living, Conscious Aging,* 80.

32 Pevny, *Conscious Living, Conscious Aging,* 80–81.

33 Palmer, *On the Brink of Everything: Grace, Gravity and Getting Old,* 2.

34 Palmer, *On the Brink of Everything: Grace, Gravity and Getting Old,* 4.

35 Robert Greenleaf, *Old Age: The Ultimate Test of Spirit – An Essay on Preparation* (Indianapolis, IN: Robert K. Greenleaf Center, 1987), 2.

36 Rupp, *The Star in My Heart,* 2.

RESOURCES

Arrien, Angeles. *The Second Half of Life: Opening the Eight Gates of Wisdom.* Boulder, CO: Sounds True, Inc., 2005, 2007.

Barr, Judith. "Persephone — Come Back from the Underworld." *News of the Sacred Work of the Feminine* (Mysteries of Life), No. 5 (1994, revised 1996): 1–2.

Bass, Diana Butler. *Grounded: Finding God in the World, A Spiritual Revolution.* New York: HarperCollins, 2015.

Berry, Wendell. "Sabbaths 1979, I." *This Day: Collected & New Sabbath Poems 1979-2013,* 7. Berkeley, CA: Counterpoint, 2013.

Boelhower, Gary J. *Choose Wisely: Practical Insights from Spiritual Traditions.* Mahwah, NJ: Paulist Press, 2013.

Bolen, Jean Shinoda. *Goddesses in Everywoman.* New York: Harper and Row Publishers, Inc., 1985.

Bridges, William. *Transitions: Making Sense of Life's Changes.* Cambridge, MA: Da Capo Press, 2004, 2019.

Bridges, William. *The Way of Transition: Embracing Life's Most Difficult Moments.* Cambridge, MA: Da Capo Press, 2001.

Bridges, William, and Susan Bridges. *Managing Transitions: Making the Most of Change.* Boston: Da Capo Press, 2016.

Brown, Brené. *Dare to Lead: Brave Work. Tough Conversations. Whole Hearts.* New York: Random House, 2018.

Brown, Brené. *Daring Greatly: How the Courage to Be Vulnerable Transforms the Way We Live, Love, Parent, and Lead.* New York: Penguin Group, 2012.

Cameron, Julia. *The Artist's Way.* New York: G.P. Putman's Sons, 1992.

Cameron, Julia. *The Artist's Way Morning Pages Journal.* New York: G.P. Putman's Sons, 1995.

Cameron, Julia, with Emma Lively. *It's Never Too Late to Begin Again: Discovering Creativity and Meaning at Midlife and Beyond*. New York: Penguin Random House, 2016.

Cloud, Henry. *Necessary Endings*. New York: HarperCollins, 2010.

Corriere, Richard, and Joseph Hart. *The Dream Makers: Discovering Your Breakthrough Dreams*. New York: Funk and Wagnalls, 1977.

D'Arcy, Paula. *Sacred Threshold: Crossing the Inner Barrier to a Deeper Love*. New York: Crossroad Publishing Co., 2004.

Duerk, Judith. *Circle of Stones*. San Diego: Lura Media, 1989.

Eliot, T.S. "East Coker." *Four Quartets*. New York: Houghton Mifflin Harcourt, 1950, 1978.

Hanh, Thich Nhat. *Living Buddha, Living Christ*. New York: Penguin Random House, 1985.

Harris, Maria. *Jubilee Time: Celebrating Women, Spirit, and the Advent of Age*. New York: Bantam Books, 1995.

Iyer, Pico. *The Art of Stillness: Adventures in Going Nowhere*. New York: Simon and Schuster, 2014.

Jarow, Rick. "The Seat of Prosperity." In *Lotus Personal Transformation*, 6, no. 1 (September–November 1996): 52–56, 79.

Jaworski, Joseph. *Source: The Inner Path of Knowledge Creation*. San Francisco: Berrett-Koehler Publishers, 2012.

Jones, Michael. *The Soul of Place: Re-imagining Leadership Through Nature, Art and Community*. Victoria, B.C.: Friesen Press, 2014.

Kula, Irwin, and Linda Loewenthal. *Yearnings: Ancient Wisdom for Daily Life*. New York: Hachette Book Group, 2006.

Lindbergh, Anne Morrow. *Gift from the Sea*. New York: Pantheon Books, 1955, 2005.

Muller, Wayne. *Sabbath: Finding Rest, Renewal and Delight in Our Busy Lives*. New York: Bantam Books, 1999.

Murdock, Maureen. *The Heroine's Journey*. Boston: Shambhala Publications,1990.

Ostaseski, Frank. *The Five Invitations: Discovering What Death Can Teach Us About Living Fully*. New York: Flatiron Books, 2017.

Paintner, Christine Valters. *The Artist's Rule: Nurturing Your Creative Soul with Monastic Wisdom*. Notre Dame, IN: Sorin Books, 2011.

Palmer, Parker. *On the Brink of Everything: Grace, Gravity, and Getting Old*. Oakland, CA: Berrett-Koehler Publishers, 2018.

Pevny, Ron. *Conscious Living, Conscious Aging: Embrace & Savor Your Next Chapter*. New York: Atria, 2014.

Pipher, Mary. *Women Rowing North: Navigating Life's Currents and Flourishing As We Age*. New York: Bloomsbury Publishing, 2019.

Pulley, Mary Lynn. *Losing Your Job – Reclaiming Your Soul: Stories of Resilience, Renewal, and Hope*. San Francisco: Josey-Bass Publishers, 2010.

Rohr, Richard, O.F.M. and The Fountain Square Fools. "Days of Renewal." Cincinnati: St. Anthony Messenger Press.

Rupp, Joyce. *Boundless Compassion: Creating a Way of Life*. Indiana: Sorin Books, 2018.

Rupp, Joyce. *The Cup of Our Life: A Guide to Spiritual Growth*. Indiana: Ave Maria Press, 1997, 2012.

Rupp, Joyce. *Open the Door: A Journey to the True Self*. Indiana: Sorin Books, 2002.

Rupp, Joyce. *The Star in My Heart*. Indiana: Sorin Books, 1990, 2004, 2010.

Schaupp, Joan. *Woman: Image of the Holy Spirit*. New Jersey: Dimension Books, 1975.

Tan, Chade-Meng. *Search Inside Yourself: The Unexpected Path to Achieving Success, Happiness (and World Peace)*. New York: HarperCollins, 2012.

Taylor, Jeremy. *The Wisdom of Your Dreams: Using Dreams to Tap into Your Unconscious and Transform Your Life*. New York, NY: Penguin, 1992, 2009.

Wagoner, David. "Lost." *Traveling Light: Collected and New Poems*. Chicago: University of Illinois Press, 1942, 1999.

Wheatley, Meg. *Perseverance*. Oakland: Berrett-Koehler Publishers, Inc., 2010.

PHOTO CREDITS

PERMISSIONS

"Sabbaths 1979, I" from *This Day: Collected & New Sabbath Poems* by Wendell Berry. Copyright ©1979 and ©2013. Published by Counterpoint Press. Reprinted by personal permission of Wendell Berry, handwritten note dated November 13, 2019.

"Persephone—Come Back from the Underworld." by Judith Barr. Published in *News of the Sacred Work of the Feminine* (Mysteries of Life), Issue Five, pp. 1–2, copyright ©1994, revised copyright ©1996. Reprinted by personal permission of Judith Barr, email and letter dated September 18, 2019.

Excerpt from *Circle of Stones* copyright ©1989 by Judith Duerk. Reprinted with permission of New World Library, Novato, CA. August 19, 2019. www.newworldlibrary.com

Excerpt from "East Coker" from FOUR QUARTETS by T.S. Eliot. Copyright ©1950 by T.S. Eliot, renewed 1978 by Esme Valerie Eliot. Reprinted by permission of Houghton Mifflin Harcourt Publishing Company. All Rights Reserved. Permission granted December 20, 2019.

Excerpts from *On the Brink of Everything: Grace, Gravity, and Getting Old* by Parker Palmer. Copyright ©2018. Published by Berrett-Koehler Publishers, Inc., quoted with the personal permission of Parker Palmer, email dated October 28, 2019.

"Lost" from *Traveling Light: Collected and New Poems*. Copyright ©1942 and ©1999 by David Wagoner. Used with permission of the University of Illinois Press dated January 9, 2020.

Excerpts from *Conscious Living, Conscious Aging: Embrace & Savor Your Next Chapter* by Ron Pevny. Copyright ©2014. Published by Atria. Quoted with personal permission of Ron Pevny, email dated August 30, 2019.

INDEX

MEET THE AUTHORS, WATCH VIDEOS AND MORE AT
WisdomfromtheWoodsBook.com

Made in the USA
Monee, IL
20 August 2020